TRAGEDY TO TRIUMPH

REULL NYGAARD WITH GUY DOUD

LifeJourney Books™ is an imprint of Chariot Family Publishing,
a div. of David C. Cook Publishing Co.
David C. Cook Publishing Co., Elgin, Illinois 60120
David C. Cook Publishing Co., Weston, Ontario
Nova Distribution Ltd., Eastbourne, England

TRAGEDY TO TRIUMPH

Cover design by Paetzold Design
Interior design by Helen Lannis and Brian Reck

First Printing, 1994
Printed in the United States of America
97 96 95 94 5 4 3 2 1

CIP Applied for.
ISBN 0-7814-1522-5

To my wife, Mary,
my sons, Scott and Kent,
my daughter-in-law, Sherry,
my three grandsons, Matthew, Nicholas, and Jonathan,
and to the memory of Kelly Jon Nygaard, my son,
I affectionately dedicate this book.
God can turn tragedy into triumph.

Joyce,

2 Cor 1:3-11

Table of Contents

PROLOGUE

If you met Reuel Nygaard today, you would probably see him as a man who has it all. He has been vice president of operations at Fingerhut Corporation, the fourth-largest catalog mail order company in the United States. He recently became chief operations officer at Parabody, a manufacturer of anaerobic fitness equipment. His stellar climb up the corporate ladder testifies to the breadth of his abilities and the depth of his commitment to a management style of servant leadership. Reuel has been married to his wife, Mary, for over thirty-five years, and he is a proud and loving father to his sons. He is a dedicated Christian who has learned to apply biblical truths to his everyday life—at work and at home.

Reuel Nygaard's entrepreneurial abilities became obvious when he was in college. He developed a small business installing deodorizers in local offices, rest rooms, and hotels. He serviced these units on a monthly basis and earned enough income to pay for his tuition, books, and room and board. Before leaving school, he sold the business to another student for one thousand dollars.

He left college after three years when he was offered a lucrative position with an optical lab where he had worked part-time. He quickly advanced through various levels of the optical business and then accepted a position at Dayton's department stores in Minneapolis. In his illustrious career with the Dayton Hudson Corporation, he rose through the ranks: manager of receiving, assistant buyer, buyer, assistant store manager, store manager, and divisional manager. In each of these positions, Reuel demonstrated tremendous ability, and the sales figures and other reports revealed his phenomenal success.

After his years with Dayton's and a brief time with the May Company in Cleveland, Reuel received a call from an old friend who was working with a new company called Cable Value Network (CVN). He quickly caught the excitement of developing a new company and joined their organization as vice president of operations. In just three years CVN grew from $150 million to over $700 million and then was sold to a competitor. One month after the buy-out, Reuel was hired by Fingerhut, where, once again, he exhibited tremendous skills and experienced great success.

From all appearances, Reuel Nygaard was living the American Dream. He had worked his way up from the bottom, a true self-made man. He had a wonderful family and a faith that sustained him.

Yes, Reuel Nygaard had it all—the American Dream.

Until one March day in 1988, when the dream shattered.

This is his story.

—Guy Doud

Chapter One

The Foundation of a Dream

My father was a Methodist minister, and I was the oldest of three children in our family. Unlike many preacher's kids, the label "p.k." didn't bother me too much. My folks did not establish unrealistic expectations for me, and most of the people in my father's churches seemed to understand my need to push the limits.

The small towns of Iowa and Minnesota I called home were good to me. Vernon Center, Minnesota, is my Lake Wobegon. Garrison Keillor might have lived there and fashioned his popular mythical village and people after the surroundings and good citizens of Vernon Center. We moved there in 1946 when my dad, Reverend Alvin Nygaard, accepted the call to pastor the local Methodist church. Vernon Center was a splendid place to practice being a kid.

Vernon Center did not escape the harsh Minnesota winters, but sliding down Charlie's hill (we thought it as towering as Everest!), skating on the frozen ponds and lakes, and building snow forts and snowmen all made winter a friend. In the spring, with hunks of ice still floating down the Blue Earth River, my friends and I would race to the river's bank to see who would be the first to plunge into its still-frigid waters. All modesty aside, I recall that I was the champ several years running.

When I was older, our family moved to Willmar, Minnesota, where I later graduated from high school. Willmar is also where I met Mary. We began dating when I was a high school senior and were married three years later.

Mary and I made a special trip to Vernon Center on our twenty-fifth wedding anniversary, a pilgrimage of sorts. I had told her so much about it, and I was eager to go back and visit the home of many of my fondest childhood memories. Ironically, the town hadn't changed a bit, and yet it had changed so much. Charlie's hill was still there, but it had shrunk considerably. And the parsonage I had considered a mansion was really just a plain, little old house. The Methodist church is still a meeting place for many of the Vernon Center faithful. As Mary and I drove by the building, I remembered many Sunday mornings when I was dressed in my Sunday finest, sitting on the hard wooden pew, listening to my father share the Good News of God's love, forgiveness, grace, and mercy.

After graduating from high school, where I had set the high school pole vault record and learned the joy of winning, I enrolled in the forestry program at the University of Minnesota. After completing my first year of school, I was uncertain about my major. I took a year off and went to Arizona to work with a crew of Hopi Indians marking timber. My foreman was a man by the name of Alvin Sague. Although he only had an eighth grade education, he was a very wise man. After observing me for several weeks, Alvin remarked, "You city folk are hurrying big for little reasons." And I was hurrying big.

It didn't take me long to figure out that I wasn't going to make much money marking timber, and Arizona was a long way from Minnesota—and from Mary. I left Arizona after about six months and returned to Minnesota, where I enrolled at St. Cloud State College to pursue a teaching degree in biology. After my junior year in college, I was offered a job as a dispensing optician at an optical company. The job paid more than I would ever make as a teacher, and so I reluctantly decided to quit college and pursue a business career. Soon I became caught in the performance trap. I felt a deep need to prove that I could be successful even without a college degree.

My father had been unhappy with some of my decisions as a young adult. Mary was a Catholic, and when we decided to get married I completed the instruction in the Catholic faith and joined her church. My dad was extremely hurt by my actions, and his recourse was his refusal to pay for my college education.

I felt I had a great deal to prove. Both my brother and sister were pursuing advanced degrees, and they both eventually earned Ph.D.'s. I, on the other hand, had not only decided not to finish college, but had left the church my father had served his entire life. All this only fueled my drivenness.

Just as my father's career had forced his family to move many times, my pursuit of different careers and opportunities did the same for my family. Unlike my father, however, I became fascinated with the power of position, the politics of career, and the potential of increased income. This fascination led to workaholism, and soon my priorities no longer reflected my true values. My numerous career moves meant physical moves for my family, and over the years I had more than a twinge of guilt that I had subjected my family to so many adjustments.

As a fifteen-year-old boy at summer camp on Lake Koronis near Paynesville, Minnesota, I had written a note on a piece of paper, signed my name, and put it in the offering plate as it passed by. The note was my pledge to the world, and to God, that I planned to live my life for Jesus. I never forgot the pledge, but I did ignore it at times. In my efforts to get ahead in the corporate world, I fell out of fellowship with God. Getting ahead seemed to necessitate socialization, which for me included lots of drinking and gambling and lifestyle choices I knew were wrong.

I became the manager of the finishing department at the lens company, which gave me opportunities to travel and attend conventions. I was living life in the fast lane. I had a reputation for telling dirty stories, and I enjoyed the socialization that was often accompanied by heavy drinking. We had a bar in the office at the optical company, and those of us in management would often gather around the bar at the end of the day. Sometimes we would leave the office and head for a local nightclub where we gambled. One night I went home with $600 I had won from a friend. I didn't feel right about the money, and I didn't feel right about how I was living. I had become insensitive to Mary's needs and the needs of my family. I went to church on Sundays, but my faith was merely a ritual and not a relationship.

Eventually my relationships at work began to deteriorate and become adversarial. I was also troubled by the lifestyle and began to look for different work. I accepted a job offer with the Dayton Hudson Company, even though it meant a move to Minneapolis and a forty percent cut in pay. Working my way up the ladder at Dayton's, I became the director of warehousing and then assistant manager of the Dayton's store in the Southdale Shopping Center, the first indoor shopping mall in America.

My career occupied about sixty-five percent of my time and energy. Mary, Scott, Kent, and Kelly received the thirty-five percent that was left. I tried my best to juggle all the responsibilities and keep my life in perspective. I tried hard to do "the right thing." I became more involved in church, serving on the building committee, the board of directors, and as a lector.

The knowledge that I did not have a college degree was always in the back of my mind. Almost everyone I knew in management had a business degree, or so it seemed. I had only a few years of college studying forestry and biology. To compensate I read every book I could find on management styles, and I especially enjoyed the biographies of those who had succeeded in business. I was surprised to find that many of the most successful business people attributed much of their success to their relationship with God, and they often quoted the Bible, chapter and verse. I had learned some Bible verses as a child, but the Bible had never become an important part of my life.

While working for Dayton's, a fellow manager kept inviting me to attend Bible Study Fellowship with him. "Reuel, you just have to come," he said again and again. I resisted, but he persisted, and finally I went. I was amazed to find 450 men from throughout the Twin Cities actively studying the Bible and applying it to their lives. I started to look forward to the Monday night meetings. The Bible became a living book, and I, too, discovered its helpful application in my life, both in my career and with my family.

One specific Bible study session significantly changed my management style. I had long realized that all those in leadership positions are given power, which I had always defined as the capacity to influence others. I also realized that power could be used or abused. As I studied a portion of Scripture from Matthew 4:1-11, I saw how Jesus came face to face with some issues of power that I had confronted as well.

> Then Jesus was led up by the Spirit into the wilderness to be tempted by the devil.
>
> And after he had fasted forty days and forty nights, he then became hungry.
>
> And the tempter came and said to him, "If you are the Son of God, command that these stones become bread."
>
> But he answered and said, "It is written, 'MAN SHALL NOT LIVE ON BREAD ALONE, BUT ON EVERY WORD THAT PROCEEDS OUT OF THE MOUTH OF GOD.'"
>
> Then the devil took him into the holy city; and he had him stand on the pinnacle of the temple, and said to him, "If you are the son of God throw yourself down; for it is written, 'HE WILL GIVE HIS ANGELS CHARGE CONCERNING YOU'; and ON THEIR HANDS THEY WILL BEAR YOU UP LEST YOU STRIKE

> YOUR FOOT AGAINST A STONE.'"
>
> Jesus said to him, "On the other hand, it is written, 'YOU SHALL NOT PUT THE LORD YOUR GOD TO THE TEST.'"
>
> Again, the devil took him to a very high mountain, and showed him all the kingdoms of the world, and their glory;
>
> and he said to him, "All these things will I give you, if you fall down and worship me."
> Then Jesus said to him, "Begone, Satan! For it is written, 'YOU SHALL WORSHIP THE LORD YOUR GOD, AND SERVE HIM ONLY.'"
> Then the devil left him; and behold, angels came and began to minister to him.

Jesus had the opportunity to use the power of his position to gain wealth, security, and personal prominence. I thought of all those I knew who had bought into the philosophy of post-Vietnam America: He who dies with the most toys wins! If the god of pleasure wasn't the one worshiped, the god of power often was. Wasn't control what life was all about? It certainly seemed that way in the world of big business.

The devil tempted Jesus, and he was tempting me as well. He took me to the pinnacle of a dream and said: "Reuel, look at all you can accomplish, all you can acquire, all you can achieve. Go for it, Reuel! Go for it!" But as I studied the Scriptures with increasing faithfulness, I realized that possessing the power to change my stones to bread did not give me the right to do so. Power is accompanied, not by freedom, but by responsibility. Jesus' management style appealed to me. Jesus was a leader, but he was first a servant. Service was primary, leadership secondary. I wanted to follow Christ's example and be a Servant Leader.

My change of management style made a tremendous difference in my behavior at home, as well as at work. Suddenly I realized that my wife was my best friend, and I became far more conscious and sensitive to Mary's needs. I wanted to serve her, too.

The next few years chronicled many changes in the life of the Nygaard family. Career advancements and opportunities took me and my family to Cleveland, Ohio, then back to Minneapolis, and finally on to LaCrosse, Wisconsin. By this time Scott had left home to attend college, and Kent was attending junior college in LaCrosse. But we were concerned about the effect our move to LaCrosse had on Kelly. He was a junior in high school, and although he didn't complain, making new friends was more difficult for him this time around. He found the students cliquish, and Mary and I sensed that he often felt lonely and depressed. We were thrilled to hear that his fellow students had elected him captain of the local hockey team after only being in the city one year. Then he got a job at the Radisson hotel, his outlook improved, and life appeared to be better for him.

❖ ❖

Through all the transitions in our lives—perhaps even because of them—we treasured our family times together. We especially enjoyed hiking and camping, and one of our favorite destinations was the north shore of Lake Superior. I remember one of the first trips we took together as a family. Kelly was just a towheaded two-year-old when we pitched the family tent on the shore of Lake Superior near Two Harbors, Minnesota. After setting up camp, we walked down to the harbor where a large ore boat was docked and was being loaded with taconite. Scott and Kent were amazed at the size of the vessel, and little Kelly seemed to be fascinated as well. I explained to the kids that the boats leave Two Harbors (or the harbors of Duluth and Superior further south) and cruise through the Great Lakes and the St. Lawrence Seaway, all the way to the Atlantic Ocean. Many of the large ships in Lake Superior are of foreign registry, and the ship workers are away from their countries and their families for months at a time. As I looked at the ships docked in the harbor, I thought of the lonely hours at sea and felt so happy to have this time of togetherness with my family.

As we walked back to the campground, Mary and I noticed the dark clouds obscuring the blue sky. We returned to our campsite, not overly concerned about what appeared to be an impending storm. We were seasoned campers and had weathered a number of nature's temper tantrums. We cooked supper, washed the dishes, and read a few stories to the children before we tucked them into bed. It wasn't long before all three of them were sound asleep. Soon the wind began to escalate, and the sides of the tent billowed like a sail. Mary and I were starting to realize that this was not an ordinary storm, when suddenly the tent's poles snapped and the canvas smothered us like plastic wrap. I tried to stand up and reach one of the boys, but the wind knocked me back to the ground. I heard a loud crack and realized that a tree had blown down, snapped in half by a mighty rush of wind. Another crack, and another tree fell. Mary and I prayed, "Dear Lord, please don't let a tree fall on us!"

As the wind continued to blow, making it impossible for me to stand to my feet, I crawled in complete darkness to reach our three kids. I found Scott. He was frightened and shaking. I managed to pull him toward Mary, who cradled him in her arms. I felt another child; it was Kent. I pulled him to Mary as well, who welcomed him to her arms along with Scott. I momentarily huddled with them before crawling away to look for Kelly. Groping blindly in the dark, I felt the end of a sleeping bag and pulled it toward me. The water was now flowing freely through the canvas, and when I finally managed to pull Kelly from his sleeping bag, his face was soaking wet. In child-like innocence, he was still sleeping soundly, oblivious to the confusion and fear of the storm wailing around us.

I found the door of the tent and carried our sleeping boy to the car. Mary followed with Scott and Kent. Quickly we packed up all of our belongings and headed home to Minneapolis. Kelly slept all the way home. The next morning when Kelly awoke, he was surprised to discover that he was in his own bed, almost two hundred miles from where he had gone to sleep. Even his two-year-old mind could understand that something strange had happened. I'm not sure, however, if he thought it strange when we bought new tent poles the same morning, dried out the tent, and headed back for the north shore the next day. It's amazing what you will do when you are young.

We were vacationing in the Black Hills of South Dakota when Kelly turned five. We all hiked up Harney Peak, the highest point in that state. The view was incredible. Two mountain goats grazed nearby, and the sky was a soft, mellow blue. The boys were as impressed with the view as we were. We stood a long time gazing across the beautiful Black Hills before heading back down to our car. As we made the descent, the sky began to turn black. Soon it was pouring rain. We were still about half a mile from the car when I shouted, "Let's run for it!" We took off like a group of sprinters running the hundred yard dash. I carried Kelly, who seemed to be enjoying the torrential downpour. When we got back to the car, out of breath and as drenched as sewer rats, Kelly looked up at me, smiled, and said, "Thanks for the birthday hike."

During Kelly's first few years in college, the two of us managed to get in a spring quarter ski trip. We stayed with my sister in Glenwood Springs, Colorado, where we had easy access to Vail, Aspen Highlands, and Sunlight, the local slope in Glenwood Springs.

Kelly mastered downhill skiing quickly, rhythmically and gracefully cruising the slopes. He made it look so easy and natural; he was fun to watch. Together we made many trips down the mountain slopes, and each descent was a special time together.

On our second trip to Colorado, we stood at the top of one of the more challenging runs at Aspen Highlands. Huge white flakes descended, without even a whisper of wind. The falling snow added even more depth to the eighteen inches of powder, and as we snaked our way repeatedly down the mountain, it was as though we were floating through a winter wonderland. When we slid to a stop at the bottom of the slope, Kelly exclaimed, "Wow! This is really awesome!" And it was.

The next run was pretty awesome, too, but for a different reason. Halfway down the slope, I leaned into my right ski and heard a loud snap. I thought perhaps I had broken one of my ski poles. I brought myself to an abrupt halt and sat down on the slope.

My skis and poles looked fine, but I felt a tremendous amount of pain in my leg. When I tried to stand up, I realized that a bone had snapped, not a ski. I descended the mountain on a toboggan, with Kelly right beside me. My sister, Gail, drove me to the hospital in Glenwood Springs, her station wagon serving as my ambulance. An orthopedic surgeon pronounced the verdict: the break was an over-extension. I had split off the right side of the tibia and needed surgery. I spent my forty-seventh birthday in the hospital, but Kelly, my sister and her children, and half of the nursing staff threw a birthday party for me. Despite the broken leg, it was one of the most special and memorable birthday celebrations of my life.

I spent the remainder of my vacation recuperating in the hospital, while Kelly divided his time between the slopes and my hospital room. He went skiing during the day with his cousin and my credit card, and at night he faithfully sat by my bed and told me all the details of each run down the slopes. I could tell, however, that he was more than a little concerned about Dad and whether I was in good spirits. This sensitivity was characteristic of Kelly; he seemed to be more concerned about other people's needs than his own.

Kelly was what I describe as a "feeler." He was always sensitive to pain in other people's lives. Their burden was his burden, and he felt frustrated that he couldn't always take his friends' burdens away. The night my father died, Kelly drove to his house shortly after he heard the news. Grandpa was eighty-eight years old, and Kelly loved him dearly. He went into the room where his grandfather's body lay on the bed. He was alone with the body for some time before the ambulance came and took Grandpa to the funeral home. When Kelly came out of the bedroom, his concern was for Grandma. He sat close to her and hugged her, and I heard him whisper to her, "You need to know that I love you, Grandma. I really love you." Kelly hurt because Grandma hurt. Her pain was his pain.

That is what I felt when he sat beside my bed as I lay in the hospital in Glenwood Springs. I got the feeling that Kelly wished that he had been the one who had broken his leg. That's simply the way he was.

❖ ❖

As I thought of all these rich memories, I realized how much I had been blessed. I had a wonderful family, and we had so many special times together. I had an exciting career that had grown as I learned to follow Christ's example. My faith in Jesus Christ provided a solid foundation on which I had built my life. My faith, my family, my career—I had it all.

The quintessential American Dream.

Until the dream became a nightmare.

CHAPTER TWO

THE DREAM BECOMES A NIGHTMARE

March is always an unpredictable month in Minnesota. Spring teases you with glimpses of summer sun, and then winter's warring cold and snow remind you that spring has not yet sprung. There are usually a few warm days in March, but often the sky seems indifferent and nondescript. A typical March day doesn't wake up, and it seems like early morning all day long. The first day of March in 1988 was this kind of day. I had looked forward to it for many months. My new job had kept me extremely busy, and I was ready for a break. Three other men from my Bible Study Fellowship group and I had planned a ski trip to Colorado. I couldn't wait to feel the powder beneath my skis. Kelly, known for his wonderful sense of humor, jokingly warned me that I had better be careful. "Remember what happened last time, Dad."

Much had happened in the last few years. I had enjoyed success in my career. I became the general manager of the St. Paul Dayton's store and served as the president of the Downtown Council of St. Paul. I was elected to the executive committee of the St. Paul Chamber of Commerce, and I tried hard to incorporate my faith and Christ's servant leader management style in all my affairs. I then left Dayton's to become the vice-president of operations for the newly established Cable Value Network, CVN, a television marketing cable network. In less than three years, sales climbed from $150 million to over $700 million.

We had moved back to Minneapolis after Kelly graduated from high school in LaCrosse. Scott was attending Hamline University majoring in pre-med, and Kent had a job with a theatrical rigging firm. Kelly had received his Associate of Arts degree from North Hennepin Community College and had just started his junior year at the University of Minnesota, the same school I had attended thirty-three years earlier.

All was going well spiritually, too. Mary and I looked for a new church after we returned to the Twin Cities, and God led us to the Evangelical Free Church in Wayzata. Our faith continued to grow and our commitment to Christ along with it. We enjoyed the straightforward inspirational messages of the pastor, John Vawter, who frequently gave the invitation for people to come to Christ and always managed to find practical application of the biblical truths. I remained involved in Bible Study Fellowship and became more and more amazed at how practical the Bible is.

I was excited about my trip with my Bible Study Fellowship friends. This trip was unusual because I was not going with anyone from my family. Mary had planned a trip to Florida with two of her best friends; Scott was preparing to take his medical board examinations in a few days; Kent was out of state on a theatrical rigging job; and Kelly had both school and work commitments. As our children grew older, it was increasingly difficult to get us all together. I didn't allow this situation, however, to affect my excitement about going skiing in Colorado. I was going with three wonderful Christian friends, and I knew that we would have a great time.

Our flight was scheduled to leave the Minneapolis/St. Paul airport at 5:00 p.m. I took the whole day off to be with Mary, who was scheduled to leave the following day for Florida. Mary and I planned a number of activities for the day. It was noon by the time we finished our errands, and we headed home to meet Kelly. Kelly had said that, if possible, he would stop by for lunch after his last class for the day. We waited at home for a while, but Kelly never came. Determining that he probably had some studying to do, we left to do a bit more shopping. We picked out a few other items we needed and then we stopped for lunch.

"I'm concerned about Kelly," I said after we had ordered. Mary looked at me and nodded. We had both been concerned for several months. Kelly had been going with the same girl for over three years. He was deeply committed to their relationship, and he always felt personally responsible for any problems that developed between them. The relationship seemed to be rocky at best, and the ups and downs seemed to drain Kelly emotionally. I tried to talk to him about his relationship. I even encouraged him to break off the relationship if it made him unhappy. His usual response was, "I'm not ready to do that right now."

Kelly had purchased concert tickets for him and his girlfriend, but they had an argument one week before the concert. When the concert date arrived, Kelly and she were not talking with one another, so it was unlikely that they would attend the concert. Instead, she took the tickets and invited another guy to go to the concert with her. Kelly was devastated. I tried talking with him again, but I made little headway. I had watched my other two boys go through broken relationships with their girlfriends, and they had survived. I was sure Kelly would survive as well. He was twenty-three, was doing well in college, and had earned praise for his job performance as a security guard. He had a host of friends, and I was certain that he would get through this crisis. Nonetheless, I could tell that the breakup was really troubling him. He wasn't sleeping well. He had lost some weight.

I was surprised one day when Mary told me that Kelly had decided to move out of our house and get an apartment of his own. I immediately sought him out.

"How can you afford to do that?" I asked, the typical father.

"Dad, I am twenty-three years old, and I'm still living at home. I need to get out and make it on my own."

A few nights later, I noticed the light on in his bedroom late into the night. When I got up at 5:00 the following morning, his light was still on. I knocked on the door, and Kelly invited me in. He was sitting on his bed, writing a letter to his girlfriend. I walked in and sat beside him.

I stared into his blue eyes. He seemed so distant. "This really bothers you, doesn't it, Kelly?"

He nodded.

"Does it help to write about it?" I asked.

"Yeah, it does," he said.

"Then I'm glad that you're writing about your struggles. It helps to not suppress your true feelings."

As we sat on the bed, I rubbed his legs and tried to get him to relax. We talked. We laughed. I left his room believing that my son was going to be okay. I only wished he could have known the same peace in this storm as he had shown over twenty years before when our tent caved in on the banks of Lake Superior.

Mary and I reviewed some of these recent events as we talked that day at lunch. Then we prayed. "Dear Lord, please watch over Kelly and calm his heart and give him peace. We pray for his relationship with his girlfriend, Dawn. We pray that your will be done, Lord. Please help Kelly work through his pain, and give him the wisdom that he needs."

After lunch we headed home to finish packing for our trips. An hour later I gave Mary a hug and a kiss good-bye and left with my friends. As we waited for our flight, I mentioned to my friends that I had asked Kelly if he would be willing to attend Bible Study Fellowship with me. He had said that he would, and so I would phone him as soon as I returned from Colorado. I shared some of the details of Kelly's life with my friends, and we decided to make Kelly a prayer priority during our week together in Colorado. I felt such blessing and support knowing that these friends shared my burden and concern.

Our flight from Minneapolis to Denver was uneventful and on time, and we quickly headed to the baggage claim area to meet our friend Jerry, who had gone to Colorado ahead of us for a few extra days of skiing. Jerry met us, but not with news of the slopes.

"When I arrived at the airport, I heard my name

being paged," he said. "I thought it was probably from you guys telling me that your flight had been delayed or something. So I answered the page and was told that there is an emergency message, and I am supposed to call this number right away. But I've been calling for ten minutes, and no one answers."

Jerry handed me a card with a name and a phone number.

"This is my neighbor," I said, with a sudden rush of fear. "Something is wrong at my house!"

I rushed to the phone and quickly dialed my home phone number. A male voice answered. The voice was familiar, but I did not immediately recognize it. "Who is this?" I demanded.

"This is John Vawter." John was our pastor, and his presence at our home confirmed my deep fear that something tragic had happened.

"John, this is Reuel. Did something happen to Mary? An accident?"

"No, Reuel, I'm afraid it's far worse than that. Kelly took his life this afternoon."

"What? You're kidding."

"I'm sorry, but there's no mistake." John spoke gently but firmly. "Reuel, your son is dead."

I was in a complete state of shock. I felt as if I had been hit with a baseball bat. I was horrified. I could not believe the news I had just received. I was overwhelmed. I couldn't even cry. Suddenly everything in my world had gone crazy. The dream was shattered. The thoughts came so quickly I could not begin to sort them out. He has to be kidding. This could not have happened to Kelly. This can't be happening to my family, to me, to Mary. This can't be true. There has to be some mistake.

"John, I want to speak with Mary."

When Mary took the phone, I was amazed at how calm she was. Had she received the same news I had just received? I realize now that Mary was in an even deeper state of shock than I was. John took the phone from Mary and told me that they had made arrangements for me to fly back to Minneapolis on the next flight out of Denver. He gave me the flight number and told me that it was the last flight out that evening. I looked at my watch and realized that I had to hurry or I'd miss it.

I could not get home fast enough. Maybe if I got home I could figure out some way to fix this whole situation, or maybe I would wake up and discover that I was having a bad dream. I ran to the counter where my friends were standing. "My son Kelly killed himself," I said. "I have to get home right away."

The woman at the flight desk screamed. I must have seemed like a wild man to her. My friends did not know what to say. They, too, were suddenly in shock. Sheer adrenaline took over. "I have to hurry, or I'll miss my plane!" I'm sure I was shouting. Soon I had a ticket in my hand and was running down the concourse toward the plane that would take me home.

When I got on the plane, my mind went completely wild. I thought again, *Once I get home I can figure out what I have to do to make this bad dream come to an end.* This was one of my strengths as a manager. I was a problem-solver, and every problem had a possible solution.

I forced myself to face the reality of what had happened, and then I was angry with myself because I had not asked for any of the details. How had Kelly done it? My mind raced with a hundred possible scenarios. *How did he kill himself? Where did he do it? Why did he end his life? How? Where? Why? The questions torpedoed through my mind. How? Where? Why?*

Then shock displaced reality again. *He isn't dead. He isn't dead. It can't be. Not Kelly. I want to cry, but I can't. And why cry when he isn't really dead? Why cry over a nightmare?*

No one on the plane knew what had happened. No one was aware of how my dream had just been shattered. *How could life be so normal for them? How could some of them laugh and go on with life as though nothing had happened? How could they be so oblivious to my pain?*

Dear God, I prayed silently in my seat, *please be with Mary. Please tell me that this isn't true. Please, God, I beg you for a miracle. Please don't let Kelly be dead!*

They were all prayers of desperation, the prayers of a desperate man who was facing a problem of tragic proportions over which he had no control. But

Reuel Nygaard never lost control. *Get me home, and I'll figure something out!*

I got off the plane in Minneapolis and headed down the concourse, not knowing who would be waiting for me. I got to the end of the causeway and saw Mary and John Vawter. I was suddenly overcome by another dose of reality. *They wouldn't be here if this had not happened. This is not a nightmare!*

Mary ran to me, and we threw our arms around one another. We stood there for a long time, holding each other.

And the tears finally came.

CHAPTER THREE

THE ORDER IS ALL WRONG

I don't know how long we stood there holding each other and crying, but I do know that I never cherished Mary's embrace more. "I love you, Mary. I love you," I told her repeatedly, and she returned my affirmation. Pastor Vawter stood by, somewhat numbed as well. Other words just did not come at first. It was as though we had to see and feel each other to confirm the fact that this was not a dream. It had happened, and it had happened to us.

Only a few hours earlier I had walked this same concourse, a man on top of the world, anticipating a few days of skiing with friends. Now I was unprepared for what the next few days would bring. I had not yet realized how my life would never be the same.

In the car on the way home, Mary described

how she heard the news of Kelly's death. "I was on the phone talking with one of my friends, making last minute plans for our trip," she said. "Then I heard someone knocking at the door. I glanced at the door, but I didn't recognize the man, so I didn't answer it at first."

"Who was it?" I asked.

"Well, he kept knocking, so I put down the phone for a minute and went to the door. He showed me his police badge, and I figured immediately that one of the boys had been in an accident. I ran back to the phone and asked my friend to come over to the house right away."

"What time was this?" I asked, feeling strangely guilty that I wasn't home with Mary to hear the news. Guilt was to become a constant companion during the next few weeks and months. *Maybe if I had... If I'd only known... Maybe we should have...*

"It was 7:00 p.m.," Mary replied.

I wanted to hear the details of Kelly's death, and yet I didn't want to hear. I wanted to know everything, but I didn't want to know anything. Learning more about the details shattered the fantasy to which I clung, the fantasy of denial that had helped me survive the flight home.

Mary continued. "The man introduced himself as a police chaplain. He was very kind." Mary started to cry. I held her.

"Did he tell you how it happened?" I asked.

"Dawn came home to her house and walked into

her bedroom. She found Kelly in her bed. He was dead."

"No," I choked. The one word was all I could say.

Mary could barely speak. "He shot himself."

The only sounds for the next few minutes were our sobs. My mind was deluged with crazy thoughts. I could not believe, would not believe, that Kelly had done such a thing. I had a million questions and a thousand ideas of what actually happened. *Maybe it had been an accident. Maybe someone shot him. Maybe... Maybe...* And then I started to feel angry because there were so many unanswered questions, so many facts we didn't know. *What type of gun did he use? Whose gun? Where did he shoot himself? How long had he been dead? Did they make any attempt to revive him? Couldn't they have done something to try to save him? How come no one heard the shot and called the police and an ambulance sooner?*

Mary shared the other details that she knew, but the details were sketchy at best. We had questions that needed answers, and we wanted the answers immediately. *Why wasn't there someone who could give us the facts now?*

"Where is Kelly now?" I asked.

"He's at the morgue," Mary said. "The funeral home will pick up his body tomorrow."

The words *funeral home* stabbed me a dozen times. Arrangements would have to be made. A casket would have to be selected. A cemetery plot would have to be purchased. And in the midst of our grief, we would have to do it all. *Just eleven months earlier I had buried my father. I would never have dreamed in my worst nightmare that less than a year later I would bury my son.*

I have never experienced such a flood of emotion. Thinking about Kelly's funeral and all the necessary arrangements left me totally numb. Shock set in again. I didn't realize then that shock was not an enemy, but rather a companion to help us survive the next few days and weeks.

I was surprised to get home and discover so many of our close friends waiting for us. A part of me wanted to withdraw and not see anyone. Withdrawal allows you to live in the fantasy of denial for a little while longer. Each familiar face you see for the first time after the tragedy is a beacon of reality that shines into the darkness of your soul where the denial lives. Facing family and friends is painful, yes, but it is necessary. I realize that it was hard for our friends, too. They would rather not have been there that night. It would have been easier for them to stay away, to withdraw as well. But as each one embraced me and cried with me, I felt the love of God himself in their arms, and no words were necessary.

One by one our friends left that first night as Tuesday evening became Wednesday morning. Eventually Mary and I were alone. We talked until three in the morning before deciding that we should go to bed and try to get some sleep. I don't think we slept at all. There were periods of momentary silence and then the stillness was broken by one of us suggesting possible explanations, questioning all over again. We still could not believe that Kelly was dead.

We were both out of bed before 7:00 a.m., finding it too difficult to stay in bed and let our minds run wild. It was easier to get busy doing something, anything that would require our attention and occupy our minds.

We hadn't been up long before there was a knock on our door. It was my cousin Bill Bruen. "I've taken a few days off," he said. "I'm here to do whatever you need me to do." We embraced, and the denial inside me screamed in anger.

Bill, along with another good friend, Chuck Wenger, spent the next two days chauffeuring us around as we made all the arrangements for Kelly's funeral. Their presence and help were invaluable.

Not long after Bill arrived, I heard another car pull up in the driveway. I looked out the window and saw our son Kent. He had been out of town and was having dinner at a restaurant when his boss found him and told him about Kelly's death. He took the first flight home, and a friend met him at the airport and brought him to our house. When we embraced and wept together in the driveway, all he could say was, "I can't believe it, Dad. I can't believe it."

And all I could say was, "I can't believe it either, Kent."

Scott planned to come home immediately after hearing about Kelly, but he was thrown a real curve when he was told that he had to take his medical board examination on Thursday as planned or he would have to wait until the following year to take it. Scott explained the circumstances. His brother had committed suicide. He needed to get home and be with his family. The state examiners, however, were unyielding and unsympathetic, so Scott had to stay in Iowa and take the test on Thursday. He arrived home later that same day.

The next several days were filled with hugs and tears. We received an outpouring of support. Peggy Gerbeling, our neighbor across the street, took charge of our house while we made arrangements. She answered the phone, took down the names of all the visitors, and helped prepare all the meals. Others stopped by with food and cards and offers of help and sympathy. Complete strangers who had also lost children through tragic circumstances stopped by. Their unspoken message was clear and helpful: you are not alone. We were not the only ones to experience this pain that seemed unbearable. Life goes on. Every hug was an exhortation that life was still worth living.

Before going to the funeral home on Wednesday, we drove to Kelly's apartment. He had lived there for only two weeks since moving out of our house. Guilt stabbed at me again. *I should have realized that his moving out was a sign of withdrawal. I should have realized that!*

We went through Kelly's closet and selected a suit for him to wear, although we weren't sure if we could have an open casket. We assumed that Kelly had shot himself in the head. We had not yet seen the body and were uncertain of how badly disfigured it was. This uncertainty fueled our grief, and our imaginations ran wild. We took Kelly's clothes with us to the funeral home, the same mortuary we used for my father eleven months earlier.

The mortician led us through the customary steps: we wrote the obituary, selected a casket, and made the arrangements for visitation. We were still uncertain, however, whether or not the casket could be open.

I finally had to ask: "Is the body badly disfigured?"

"No, not at all," the mortician answered. "He shot himself in the chest."

Mary and I were surprised and relieved. We have since wondered why we immediately assumed that he had died from a head wound. With this fact now known, we told the mortician that we wanted an open casket.

Bill and Chuck drove us to the cemetery to select a plot. Mary and I looked at several available plots and chose a grassy spot at the top of a little hill that overlooked a stand of trees. "Kelly would like this spot," Mary said.

"It reminds me of some of our camping trips together," I replied.

We stood for a while and looked at the three burial plots we had just purchased. Someday Mary and I will be buried next to Kelly there on that little hill. As we stood there, death confronted me again. I knew death was part of life, but like most people I kept the knowledge of it in the archives of my mind, hoping not to confront it. When death occurs, as it certainly will, we experience incredible pain because we have lulled ourselves into believing that it will not happen to us. Everyone believes that they and their loved ones are going to live at least one more day. But as I stood holding Mary's hand, I realized that in our case, the order was wrong. Children are supposed to bury their parents.

Wednesday we also went to our church in Wayzata to meet with John Vawter. He had been such a source of comfort to us. We met in his office at the church and visited for a few moments, filling him in on the arrangements we made with the mortician. Then John asked, "What do you want to come from this funeral?"

The question made us think, and after a few minutes Mary summarized our thoughts. "We want Kelly to be honored. We want God to be glorified. And we want everyone who comes to the funeral to hear the gospel message."

Pastor Vawter smiled gently as he jotted down a few notes.

"Kent and Scott both want to say a few words at the funeral," I said. "They want to eulogize their brother." I knew that God would need to give both of them a special gift of strength. Before we left Pastor Vawter's office, we prayed again, and we prayed that God would give Scott and Kent the strength to endure and the words to speak.

Thursday morning I walked out and picked up the paper in the mailbox. It was another one of those indifferent March days. I brought the paper into the house and set it on the kitchen table. Mary came down for breakfast and began to read the paper. I heard her gasp softly, and then she began to cry.

"What is it, Mary?"

"Kelly's obituary," she said, holding the paper so I could see his name in print. *Kelly Jon Nygaard. Born August 1st, 1964. Died March 1st, 1988.* I read the obituary with Mary, and we held each other and wept together. Seeing his name on that page struck a blow for reality, but once again shock and disbelief came to the rescue.

The greatest reality, however, came the next day when we went to the funeral home to see Kelly's body for the first time. As I reflect on the experience now, I realize that the anxiety was worse than the actual episode. There was actually something assuring about seeing him so at peace. Of course, it caused tremendous grief to see that he actually was dead; but the sooner the reality of death is accepted, the sooner the healing process can begin.

The initial fear of seeing the body soon gave way to a multitude of thoughts and feelings. Each thought and feeling is an important step in the healing process. As Kent and Scott and Mary and our loved ones visited at the funeral home, we shared fond memories and even laughed occasionally as we remembered many of the good times. Kelly loved well and was well loved. He had a tremendous sense of humor that brought joy into each of our lives.

Over five hundred people stopped by the funeral home. I couldn't believe all the people. Carloads came from communities where we used to live. Friends of Kelly's whom we did not even know came and shared stories of what a special friend he had been to them. Some of his fellow employees told us they often waited until Kelly signed up for a shift so they could choose the same shift as they enjoyed working with him. One of Kelly's friends said to me, "Mr. Nygaard, Kelly always had such a happy disposition. He was a bunch of fun. I loved being with him. I can't believe that he killed himself. I can't believe it. Why did he do it? *Why?*"

The same question would consume me for many months to come. *Why?*

CHAPTER FOUR

I MUST TELL JESUS

Reuel, Mary, Scott, Kent and Sherry, Grandmother Nygaard, I wish we weren't here today."

Pastor Vawter stood behind the pulpit and began the funeral. He looked right at us. How many times had I watched and listened to him from behind that same pulpit? I had heard him preach sermons about real faith, sermons that stressed that we are to thank God and rejoice in every situation. I could not believe that Pastor John could possibly tell us to rejoice today.

"I really hurt for you all." John paused to maintain his composure. His words were simple but so helpful. Shared tears said more than words. Those who cried with us spoke volumes. Yet seeing that Kelly's death had brought pain into hundreds of lives brought another kind of guilt, strange feelings of responsibility, and the desire to make everyone happy again.

"Reuel and Mary," he continued, "you have entered a very select group—the fraternity of parents who lose their children. Many people in this church are in that fraternity. And except for God himself, they, more than anyone, can touch your lives now. So let them do that. Now let's pray together."

All of us in the congregation bowed our heads for prayer, and as we did, I thought of John's statement. *Mary and I have entered a select fraternity. That's one way of looking at it. But it is a fraternity no one would ever choose to belong to, and I wanted out of it!*

Many people in the church have lost their children? How many? Is it possible that others have known a similar grief? Have I been oblivious to others' pain?

"Father, we know that you don't have a best side because you're perfect, but it seems like we see your best side during times like these. Maybe it is because we are more sensitive to you, more attuned to you. I pray for all here who grieve, that you would be close to them. You are the God of all comfort. I pray that you would comfort them, particularly Reuel and Mary. I pray today as we spend these few moments together that you will allow us to make sense out of all that has transpired. And we pray this in Christ's name. Amen."

John's prayer shot another cannonball at my wall of denial. *This is the funeral. This is really happening. We are burying our son, our Kelly. Can any sense be made from all of this?* I consciously desired an understanding, but subconsciously I doubted that it would ever be possible.

We stood to sing the hymn that Mary had selected. The song was the first to come to Mary's mind as we considered congregational music for the funeral. Mary said that the words to this song expressed her feelings, our feelings. The organ prelude to the song complete, we all began to sing:

> I must tell Jesus all of my trials, I cannot bear these burdens alone;
> In my distress He kindly will help me,
> He always loves and cares for His own.

As we got to the chorus of the song, the tears flowed freely, and Mary and I held hands as we sang:

> I must tell Jesus! I must tell Jesus! I cannot bear my burdens alone;
> I must tell Jesus! I must tell Jesus! Jesus can help me, Jesus alone.

These words have come to Mary and me thousands of times since that day.

> I must tell Jesus all of my troubles, He is a kind, compassionate friend;
> If I but ask Him, He will deliver, Make of my troubles quickly an end.

Really? Could Jesus make all of our troubles come quickly to an end? I don't know if I wondered this during the funeral, but I did later. At that moment I clung to whatever faith I had, wanting desperately to believe that it was enough to help me endure and survive this crisis. The image of Christ being my kind, compassionate friend sustained me, and I pictured a loving Jesus who really did want me to tell him all of my troubles, and a Savior who was willing to bear all my burdens. It would be months, however, before I would be able to identify all that I was feeling—and months more before I could express my doubt and my anger. Only then would I really understand what a kind, compassionate friend Jesus really is.

Several years later I heard the story behind the song *I Must Tell Jesus*, which was first published in 1894. Elisha A. Hoffman was a pastor and a composer of over 2,000 gospel songs. He was pastoring a church in Lebanon, Pennsylvania, when one day he stopped to call on a lady whom he visited frequently. According to Pastor Hoffman, this woman had known much sorrow and had become very discouraged. She shared her heartache and her burdens, and then she looked Pastor Hoffman in the eyes and asked, "Brother Hoffman, what shall I do? What *shall* I do?"

Pastor Hoffman answered, "You cannot do better than to take all of your sorrows to Jesus. You must tell Jesus."

The woman thought for a moment, and then, according to the story, her eyes lit up and she said, "Yes, I must tell Jesus."

Pastor Hoffman went home and wrote the words and the music to the song—the song that almost a hundred years later would be sung at Kelly's funeral. The woman whom Pastor Hoffman visited, who had known much pain and sorrow, probably never knew how God had used her pain to be a source of comfort to millions of others.

But I didn't know this story on that March day as we sang the chorus one last time:

> I must tell Jesus! I must tell Jesus! I cannot bear my burdens alone;
> I must tell Jesus! I must tell Jesus! Jesus can help me, Jesus alone.

"Please be seated," Pastor Vawter continued. "Kelly's brothers, Kent and Scott, would like to eulogize their brother, and they are going to do so at this time." Pastor John paused just a moment before continuing. "This is difficult for them, and they may get emotional. Remember that tears have nothing to do with how macho you are; in fact, tears are healing. So I ask your indulgence if they need a moment to compose themselves."

Mary and I had prayed for this moment. We knew it would not be easy for Scott and Kent. They had shared their eulogies with the family the night before, and on each attempt they broke down. Nevertheless, they were both determined that they wanted to say good-bye to their brother at the funeral, and so Mary and I promised that we would be praying for them when they stepped to the pulpit.

Scott went first. He looked at the large crowd assembled and said, "I just want to thank all of you for coming to pay tribute to our brother, Kelly."

Scott recalled some of the good times we had shared together as a family, and then he read from a couple of letters we had received after Kelly's death. One letter was from a scoutmaster who had worked closely with Kelly. Scott read from the man's letter:

Over the years I have worked with over 400 young men in the Boy Scouts, Explorers, and other youth organizations. Over all those years and all those young people, I still regard

> *your son Kelly as being one of the five best young men I have had the pleasure and privilege to work with. Kelly's attitude, his willingness to help others, and his character set him far above his peers. I hope it is a small measure of comfort to you to know that in at least two cases that I know of, Kelly made a positive difference in another life. Although I haven't seen Kelly in many years, I will miss him.*

It was good to hear this testimony, but it was like throwing gas on the fire of my anger and confusion. *Why did such a fine young man as this take his life?*

Kelly had been a security guard at the City Center in downtown Minneapolis and had received much praise for his work. Scott concluded by reading from a letter that Kelly's boss had received from some thankful patrons:

> *Our car was broken into, and a theft occurred. Kelly, the security guard on duty, deserves recognition for his help and concern for us in this matter. He went out of his way in helping us, and he deserves to be recognized. We would like to thank Kelly for all of his help and wish there were more people like him in this world.*

By this time Scott was struggling to hold back the

wave of emotion, but God gave him the added strength he needed to make his closing statement. "Well, I think that's really who Kelly was to me. I'm thankful to the Lord for twenty-three years and all the people's lives he touched, including mine."

Why? My mind began repeating the question like a litany. *Why? Why?*

Kent began his remarks by reading from another letter Mary and I received after Kelly's death:

> *Dear Mr. and Mrs. Nygaard, Kelly saved my life. I was working security at the City Center, and a man pulled a knife on me. Kelly backed me up. If he hadn't, I would not be here. He was a great man.*

Then *why?*

Kent followed with another letter:

> *Kelly was liked and loved by all his fellow employees at City Center. He wasn't a common guy. He was different. He seemed to get more out of life than many others. He always had a smile for you. He always put you in a good mood if you were down. Kelly will never be forgotten by myself or the rest of the department. We've hung Kelly's picture in our office. Now I can still come in and look up at it and know deep inside that I'm working with*

Kelly today. Although it may put a tear in my eye, I'll have a smile on my face 'cause that's the kind of guy he was.

I couldn't stop the tears now. *So why?*

Kent had made it through; our prayers for him and Scott had been answered. He looked toward the congregation and said, "Once again, Scott and I thank you for your warmth in paying tribute to our brother Kelly." Then he looked toward Kelly's casket and concluded: "Good-bye, brother. Good-bye, our best friend. We love you. May you rest in peace with the Lord's comfort."

Although it was therapeutic to say it, and I said it many times myself, "good-bye" has an empty ring if there is no one there to hear you say it. In a suicide, there is no good-bye.

"He was always willing to listen and to help; he just had a hard time sharing with others when he needed help, when he was in pain," John continued in his funeral meditation. "I guess the best way to say it is that near the end of his life, his strengths of sensitivity and caring for others actually became his weakness."

During the days between Kelly's death and the funeral, all of us close to him had spent hours recalling his many acts of kindness, his strength of caring, as Pastor John put it. Grandma Nygaard unabashedly admitted that, of all her grandchildren, Kelly was her favorite. Kelly had stopped by her house at least once a week to check on her and help himself to some of the goodies in her refrigerator, a raid that Grandma cherished. He took good care of her lawn, making sure it was always mowed, while Grandma, age eighty-six, cooked one of his favorite meals.

Pastor Vawter took many of these recollections and incorporated them into his message and spoke directly to each of us close to Kelly. "Reuel and Mary, the young man who took his life was not the young man we all knew. His sensitivity got the best of him. He began reacting to life with his heart instead of thinking with his head. So I encourage you to remember twenty-three great years—not one irrational act. The twenty-three years are what made the man, not the act."

They were words that helped, they really did. But I knew I needed a more complete explanation soon in order to try to put everything into perspective. Simply saying that his sensitivity got the best of him left too many questions unanswered, questions I had to answer if I was ever going to have peace.

Pastor Vawter now addressed Kelly's former girlfriend. I had thought of how horrible it must have been for her to come home and find him dead in her bed. Although I had an intellectual understanding of her trauma, my pain was so great that I had many unresolved feelings concerning Dawn. I had encouraged Kelly to break up with her and date someone else, and I wondered for the umpteenth time if he would still be alive if he had followed my advice. Despite the unresolved feelings, I did have compassion for Dawn, and I grieved this circumstance that would forever bind us together with its tragic memory.

"Dawn, your spirit is crushed. It would be easy to overlook you during this time of tragedy and pain. But I want you to know, Dawn, that the Nygaards reach out to you. And although you're not officially family, you are in their hearts. It's important for you to know that, particularly on this day."

Pastor John turned to Kent and Scott. "You are experiencing the pain that has no name," he said. "Let me encourage you to turn to God in a whole new way. Let him do with your lives whatever he wants to do because of this pain."

John then shared, from 2 Corinthians 2, The Apostle Paul's explanation of how God comforts us in our affliction so that we might comfort others in their affliction. He encouraged everyone to learn from Kelly's life, not to sit idly by if we see someone in pain.

John had put together a service that both Mary and I felt met the criteria we had established: "We want Kelly to be honored. We want God to be glorified. And we want everyone who comes to the funeral to hear the gospel message of salvation preached." He minced no words when he shared the message of salvation.

"It would be a double tragedy today if we were this close to God and thinking this profoundly about God, and yet didn't meet him. So the family has asked me to encourage all of us to rethink. Do we know God in a personal way?"

Then John shared the A,B,C's of life. "Knowing God is as easy as A, B, C. First, A: Admit that we are imperfect and sinful. B: Believe that Jesus Christ died for our sins and that he wants to come into our lives and live through us. C: Confess our sins and actually invite him into our lives."

The church was filled with people—family, close friends, and friends of friends. Mary and I had no idea where these people were in their journey of faith, but we wanted Kelly's death to remind people of the brevity of life and the reality of an eternal destiny. Even though Kelly took his life, we knew that he had known Jesus, and we believed that he was with Jesus. We wanted everyone to know that blessed assurance.

"So let me encourage you in the privacy of your thoughts, if you've never met God, to admit your imperfection and your sinfulness, to believe that he died for your sin, and to believe that he wants to come into your life, and finally, to confess your sin and invite him in. Pray silently a prayer something like this: "Dear Jesus, I admit my sinfulness and my imperfections. I believe that you died on the cross for me and that you want to live in me. Now I invite you into my life."

I later learned that at least one young person had prayed the prayer along with Pastor Vawter and asked Christ into her life.

I've reread the manuscript of John's message many times since that March day in 1988. Although I heard all the words the first time, I was still numb, still somewhat in shock, and the complete reality of what had happened was not yet apparent. Faith, friends, and family sustained me. A million issues still needed resolution. Again came the haunting question: *Why?* I struggled, wanting to be strong for my children and for Mary. I wanted to be strong for me. I wanted to be strong while everything on the inside felt weak, all too human, ready to collapse.

God must have given Pastor Vawter these words to say: "God's power is perfected in us when we are weak. There is no sin in being weak. There is no sin in being brokenhearted. Let me encourage you to allow God to touch your life during this time of tragedy."

As I stood holding Mary's hand on the little hill at Lakewood Cemetery, I had never been more conscious of how weak I really was.

I must tell Jesus. I cannot bear these burdens alone!

Chapter Five

Confronting the *Whys?*

We opened the door and slowly entered the apartment. We were still in shock, functioning mechanically, doing what we needed to do.

Denial and reality played games with my mind. Denial whispered to me as I opened the door to Kelly's apartment, "I wonder if he's home." Reality screamed back, "You fool, he's not home. He's dead. He killed himself, remember? You'll never see him again!"

We started to pack Kelly's things. I was thankful that Kent and Sherry and Scott were able to help Mary and me with the work. I walked over to his desk and reached for some of the books to put into a box. And then I saw a letter lying there. "Dear Kelly, Soon you will be off to college, and the decisions you make from here on out will affect the rest of your life." I picked up the letter and stood reading it. Suddenly I remembered the night in 1982 when I had written this letter to Kelly. I was in New York City on business, and I sat in the hotel alone, thinking about the tremendous pride I felt for each of my children. Kelly was about to graduate from high school, and I wondered if I had adequately expressed my deep love and affection for him. I felt led to write Kelly a letter, just as I had done for my other two sons. Had he re-read it shortly before he died?

"Look at this," I called to the family. When they had gathered around, I read the letter aloud.

Dear Kelly,

Soon you will be off to college, and the decisions you make from here on out will affect the rest of your life. I thought you might be interested in your father's capsule view of the past eighteen years.

I remember the pride I felt when my third son was born—a pride that continued to grow as I watched you grow from baby to boy to young man. I watched a caring, friendly personality develop. You began to understand goals and the self-satisfaction of achieving them. You also learned to adjust to change when we moved to different cities. Tough going didn't make you quit, though, and it wasn't long before your self-confidence demonstrated your ability to adjust. New friends were found, responsibility taken when you got a job, and leadership qualities surfaced when you were elected captain of the hockey team. Yes, the normal boy inquisitiveness showed forth and you experimented with the normal things (smoking, parties, alcohol, etc.) but you emerged from each experience more mature. Another way of stating it would be to say that you learned from your mistakes.

I also appreciate your comfort level in bringing your friends home. Your friends have been our friends, and your choice is top drawer. Your finding a job and being willing to work shows that you have ambition, and your attendance record indicates that you are reliable. You have developed strong personal qualities and are well on your way to success.

I've seen you continue to maintain an interest in your faith. My prayer is that you will also continue to grow in this area. In my own life, faith in Jesus Christ was the final link that completed the chain and really makes all the other things happen. The Bible is filled with real life applications; I would recommend that you read from it on a regular basis.

I hope this letter helps you know that you have been a joy to have as a son the past eighteen years, and I'm very proud of the man that I see you becoming. I know I speak for your mother as well, and you have my contin-

ued support as you begin your college career.
Kelly, thanks for being you.

I Love You,
Dad

P.S. I'm proud I have you as a son.

When we finished reading the letter, I know we were all thinking the same thing: how could the young man described in this letter take his own life?

❖ ❖

Packing up Kelly's things that day was a victory for reality in its war with denial. The funeral should have been a victory for reality as well, but I'm not sure that it was. Kelly seemed so alive as Scott and Kent and Pastor John talked about him. Hundreds of friends and family members had surrounded us with such an outpouring of emotion. They had filled that first week after Kelly's death with so much love that there had been no room to get in touch with the full measure of our grief. The phone rang constantly. The mailbox was filled with cards. The kitchen table and counters were piled with food that people had delivered, knowing we had no energy to cook for ourselves. But now the funeral was over. The phone was silent for long periods of time. The cards soon stopped coming. It was back to the normal routine of life, except now that the shock had worn off, reality took my hand and asked me to dance.

The dance began the first day after the funeral. It was a new dance. Nothing was normal anymore. Nothing was routine. That first day was the first of many firsts. I soon realized that there was a first of everything. Just a month after Kelly's funeral was the *first* Easter without him. Then came the *first* birthday, the *first* summer, the *first* new school year, the first Thanksgiving, the *first* Christmas, followed by a thousand other *firsts*. Sometimes I began to question my sanity. Did everything have to be the first? Even seemingly trivial things took on monumental significance. This is the *first* summer I won't watch Kelly water ski. This is the *first* time we'll go to a movie and not be able to tell Kelly about it. I was angered by these thoughts and wished they'd go away, but they did not.

Not only were there thousands of firsts, but for each *first* there was a *last:* the *last* time I watched Kelly water ski, the *last* time we went to church together, the *last* time we went fishing. The *last* time...

Mary and I were invited to a wedding not long after Kelly's death—our first wedding since the funeral. The joy in the church was apparent. The young couple stood before the altar, obviously high on the feelings of committed love. I was happy for them. But then a tidal wave of emotion overtook me: *I'll never have the chance to see my son married.* I looked at Mary beside me in the pew. The wave had overtaken her, too.

These waves came crashing in unexpectedly. One day Mary was shopping for groceries and saw one of Kelly's favorite foods on the shelf, and the wave came. Other little things would remind me of Kelly, and I would react before I knew what was happening.

I discovered that there is no prescribed order to grief. It is not stable. It is not predictable. It is a process. Emotional outbursts are expected after such a tragedy, and they are totally acceptable, even necessary. I gave myself permission to feel what I felt. I realized that I could not deny the pain I was feeling. It was normal. If life was to go on, I had to come to terms with the pain. That is part of the grief process. I never knew when these feelings would invade me, but sadness was always standing in the wings ready to enter whenever I was reminded of my love for Kelly.

Exactly one week after Kelly's funeral, the phone rang at our house. Mary answered it.

"Is Kelly there?" asked the female caller.

"Who is this?" Mary asked.

"I'm one of Kelly's professors at the university, and I've missed Kelly in class. I wondered if he is sick and if he will be coming back to class soon."

Mary didn't blame the professor, but how was it possible that she hadn't heard? Mary felt like I did—we wanted the whole world to stop and grieve with us.

The professor continued. "A part of the grade

for our class is based on attendance. Kelly is getting an A so far, and I hate to see him jeopardize his grade."

The words didn't come easily for Mary. "Kelly killed himself last week."

The professor was shocked. After a moment she told Mary that on Tuesday, the day of Kelly's death, he came to class and made a presentation. It was well-prepared, as she said all of Kelly's class work was. "I'm so sorry, Mrs. Nygaard. I had no idea. Kelly was such a special student, and he added so much to my class. He received an A on his presentation last Tuesday. I talked with him for about ten minutes after class. He was as pleasant and friendly as always. I simply can't believe it. I can't believe it."

Kelly had left that class at 10:15 Tuesday morning, and by 2:30 p.m. he was dead. What had happened between 10:15 and 2:30? And why?

This encounter was the first of many that created uncomfortable situations for us and others. Each encounter reminded us again of the pain that was always waiting to return.

"Let God do with your lives whatever he wants to do because of this pain." Pastor Vawter's words echoed in my mind. I wasn't really sure at this point what God wanted to do with my life, but I knew what I had to do: I had to find some answers to the questions that blanketed my mind.

Of all the questions, the one that hit first and

lingered the longest was the question *why?* Not only did I ask, *Why Kelly?* I also shouted the question, *Why me?*

Kelly was obviously much more desperate than I had realized. I knew he had been depressed, but I viewed depression as a temporary experience caused by some unfortunate circumstances. I had experienced depression. Hadn't everyone? Life wasn't always wonderful. What was the old saying? *You have to take the bitter with the sweet.* I knew that Kelly was troubled by the breakdown in his relationship with Dawn, but I was confident that his sadness was temporary and that soon he would be back to his old jovial self.

In my search to better understand all the whys, I began to read whatever I could find about depression. I was surprised to discover the difference between depression and sadness. Sadness comes and goes according to the events and circumstances that occur. Depression, however, lingers on and weighs heavily. Depression is marked by sadness, but by a sadness that seems inescapable. If sadness lingers and crisis is added to crisis, trial added to trial, chemicals in the brain are often affected.

At this point depression is no longer merely the product of one's circumstances; it is a brain disease caused by a chemical imbalance. The brain can no longer regulate itself, and chemicals such as serotonin and norepinephrine are depleted or are rendered inactive. Unless the chemical imbalance is corrected, depression will most likely continue. Anti-depressant medication is often necessary to correct the chemical imbalance, and psychotherapy is used to treat any underlying psychological conflicts. In severe cases of depression, electric shock therapy may be used. Whatever the case, depression is a serious illness that, left untreated, can often result in death. In fact, 15% of all the people who become acutely depressed and do not receive the treatment they need take their own lives.

As I read and studied more about depression, I realized that Kelly was one of the more than 11 million Americans who suffer from major depression. And he was one of the 15% who choose to end their lives.

Some people die from heart disease. Some die from cancer, a disease that invades many different parts of the body. Kelly had died from an untreated brain disease. On his own power and in his own strength, he was completely incapable of stopping the advancement of the disease, and the disease finally engulfed him.

I continued to study and learn more about this hideous, misunderstood disease which often goes undetected. Kelly had all the classic signs. He had come to believe that he had little to look forward to and that he was a failure. Many of these feelings originated because of significant losses he had experienced. He found it difficult to sleep at night. He lost weight. He withdrew from those close to him. He lost interest in many of the activities he used to enjoy. As I read the list of depressive symptoms, I was consumed again with guilt. *How could I have been so blind? Why didn't I grasp how seriously depressed Kelly was?*

I heard a psychologist describe suicide as "the elimination of alternatives." He said, "The person who commits suicide has often been so depressed that he or she gradually dissolves in the pain and the future becomes intolerable. No other alternatives seem to exist. Suicide seems to be the only way out."

Had Kelly really eliminated all of his alternatives? I wondered. Why hadn't he come to Mary and me for help? Wasn't that a possible alternative? I realized, however, that Kelly had eliminated that alternative, and in the course of my therapy and grief counseling, I came to understand why. It wasn't because he felt Mary and I would not help him. He knew we were there for him. But he obviously felt that he did not want to burden anyone else with his problems. He cared so much for others and their feelings that the thought of imposing his problems on someone else—especially those he loved most—wasn't even a consideration.

How could he have thought this way? It actually made me angry to think that Kelly, in his desire not to burden me, had taken his own life and had saddled me with a weight that seemed impossible to bear. He hadn't contemplated how profoundly his suicide would change my life, our lives. *How could this disease called depression be so deceptive as to lead someone to believe that death was the best solution? How absurd!*

I was angry. I was angry at Kelly, but I couldn't admit it. *How could I be angry at this precious child of mine who had endured such pain? I should be ashamed of myself!* I stuffed the anger back down inside. I'd have to work through it later.

I frequently studied the list of depressive symptoms, many of them characteristic of Kelly's last few months. I concluded that many depressive symptoms are related to losses in a person's life. Kelly had lost Dawn, but who or what else? Together Mary and I and other family members recalled the last eighteen months of Kelly's life, and we realized that this sensitive young man had experienced a tremendous amount of loss in a short period of time.

One night Kelly was at home, and we were enjoying each other's company and watching television. The phone rang, and Kelly jumped up to answer it. "Oh, no... Oh, no..." Shock and disbelief showed in his voice and on his face. "Oh, no..." he kept repeating. When he finally hung up the phone, he came to us and said simply, "Jeff and Mike both drowned today while they were duck hunting." Jeff and Mike were two of his closest friends.

Mary and I knew that Kelly was overtaken by grief. He became strangely quiet. He avoided talking about it and sidestepped our attempts to get him to express his feelings. He was asked to do the eulogy at one of the funerals, and he spent hours looking for an appropriate poem to share. It was important to him to find just the right poem with the right words, and he seemed almost obsessed in his search.

Shortly after the funerals for Jeff and Mike, we received a letter from friends in Cleveland, where I had managed a store for the May Company. We were always glad to keep in touch with friends. The letter, however, brought more sad news, especially for Kelly. While in Cleveland, Kelly had played baseball for a city team. Kelly was the catcher on the team, and Duke, his best friend and neighbor, was the leading pitcher. Kelly and Duke were inseparable. I'll never forget the day the letter arrived and I had to share its contents with Kelly.

"Kelly, I have some sad news to share with you," I said.

He just stared at me. "What is it?" he asked finally.

"Duke died from leukemia."

I saw the same look of shock and disbelief on his face that I had seen when he heard the news of Jeff and Mike. And again he was speechless and would not talk about it.

After both tragedies, however, he continued to function, to carry on. There were slight changes in his disposition, but nothing led me to suspect that he was becoming severely depressed. Kelly, I believe, tried to hide his depression the best he could. And he was quite successful. His marvelous sense of humor was a mask that covered the real Kelly who was torn apart on the inside, carrying so much pain that he could not face it. His total absorption in other people's needs caused him to short-change himself and consider himself unworthy of similar concern from others.

And then Grandpa died.

Kelly was so concerned about Grandma. I've already shared how he sat next to her, embracing her, saying "Grandma, you need to know that I love you." At Grandpa's funeral, Kelly, representing all the grandchildren, read the same poem that he had read at Jeff's funeral.

As we looked back over those eighteen months, we saw another loss that hit Kelly hard. Kelly loved animals and had many pets. He grew up with gerbils, snakes, fish of all kinds, and an iguana. He even had a pet white rat that slept with him. He showed love for all his pets, but George was his favorite. This Labrador-German Shepherd mix shared Kelly's life for over sixteen years. She was with him through all the transitions, from Minneapolis to Cleveland to Minneapolis to LaCrosse and back to Minneapolis. George was as much a part of the family as anyone. But George had been growing old. Each day George lost more and more control. It was obvious that it was only a matter of time before she would have to be put to sleep, although none of us admitted this easily. Finally, we had a family conference. It was an emotional decision for all of us, but George was miserable and we all agreed that it was time for her to go.

"I'll take George to the vet, " Kelly said.

"Are you sure?" I asked. I knew that Kelly was deeply attached to the dog, and although we would all miss George, I knew Kelly would be most deeply affected.

"I'll take her," Kelly repeated firmly.

Before leaving for the vet, Kelly gave George a bath and groomed her one more time. When he was finished, we all said good-bye to George, and then Kelly drove off to the vet. An hour or so later he came home. He didn't say a word, but he carried George from his car out into the garden where he had dug a grave.

Weeks later as we were discussing George, I said, "Kelly, I don't know how you did it."

"I'll never go through that again," was all he said.

Many months went by before he could even talk about George. When Kelly did, all he said was, "She died in my arms."

Looking back at these events, knowing what I now know about depression, I realize that Kelly never completely recovered from these losses. Each loss was like an ocean of water poured into a barrel that was already overflowing. These losses, along with his breakup with Dawn, were all factors that dug a pit of depression into which he fell and did not escape.

I now had a better understanding of why suicide, but I still couldn't understand why *me?*

Pastor Vawter made the statement at the funeral that Kelly's sensitivity had gotten the best of him. "He began reacting to life with his heart instead of thinking with his head." Depression will do that to an individual. In fact, the depressed person is often incapable of any rational thought.

"Remember twenty-three great years," Pastor Vawter had said. "Don't remember one irrational act." Understanding that Kelly had a brain disease helped me understand the irrational act and allowed me to concentrate on the twenty-three great years. The Kelly I knew was a caring, compassionate young man. I still can see him searching to find the right poem for Jeff's funeral. I still can hear him reading it at my dad's funeral. The poem was so appropriate that Mary and I included it in Kelly's memorial folder. It is a poem by Helen Steiner Rice entitled *He's Only Gone On.*

At last his gallant soul
took flight
into the land
where there is no night...
But his name is carved
in our hearts to stay

as we think of the things
that he used to say...
So he is not dead,
he's only gone on
Into a brighter,
more wonderful dawn...
For men like him
were not born to die
But, like the sun
that shines in the sky,
They warm the earth
and the hearts of men
And in happy remembrance
they live again...
So while he sleeps
and his voice is still,
His spirit goes on
and it always will.

Yes, Kelly's spirit lives on, and it always will.

As we sorted through Kelly's clothes, books, and possessions that day in his apartment, I opened one of the bags in the closet. I found George's dog collar and tags and a bag of George's hair.

Chapter Six

Learning to Lean

I got out of my car feeling quite apprehensive. I held Mary's hand as we headed for the church. *This takes lots of guts,* I thought. *Coming here is an admission that I need some help in dealing with my grief. But do I really? Am I not strong enough to handle it on my own? Is my faith in God too weak to sustain me? Doesn't God help those who help themselves?*

We were about to enter the church when another couple greeted us. "Good evening. Is this your first time here?" They smiled warmly. *What possible grief had they known in their lives?*

"Yes," Mary and I responded simultaneously.

"Well, we're glad you came. Come on in, and we'll show you where we meet."

This *Survivors of Suicide* group had been recommended to us by a grief counselor that Mary and I had seen. After the shock wore off and the hard, cold reality set in, Mary and I realized that we were experiencing some of the same signs of depression that had plagued Kelly. We sought out a counselor, and he recommended this group.

I had questions about therapy groups, but I had almost no firsthand experience. I knew that the purpose of such groups was for people to supply mutual support for one another and to create a safe environment where it was acceptable for members to share their deepest feelings. I had heard that not only was it okay to cry, but tears were common. But I wasn't sure if I could be that emotionally honest. My father's Scandinavian blood ran through my veins, and although I had cried a million tears already, I still tried to act strong when everything inside felt like it was falling apart. I needed to keep up the appearance of having it all together.

I looked at the twenty or so folks who began to take their seats in a circle in the fireside room of the church. Had all of them lost someone they loved to suicide?

I held a little pamphlet in my hand and quickly skimmed its contents. *100 people kill themselves each day.* I found that nearly impossible to believe. *Suicide is the third leading killer among young people.* I looked away from the pamphlet to those seated in the circle. Was this that "special fraternity" to which John Vawter had alluded in his funeral message?

The group facilitator spoke. "Well, it's seven o'clock, so I think we will get started. Let's go around the circle and introduce ourselves. We'll start to my right."

A middle-age lady in a red dress spoke. "Hi, my name is Joyce. My husband Rolf shot and killed himself last year. This group has been such a source of support and comfort for me."

Everyone said, "Hi, Joyce." You could hear the love in the voices.

I sensed that these people could help me, knew they would understand. But still I struggled to open up and let them. One thought kept repeating in my mind:

What am I doing here?

❖ ❖

After the cards and calls and cakes and carnations quit coming, everyone expects life to be normal again. But it isn't until that moment when you are expected to *get on with life* that you realize how different life is, and the true grief process begins. A death like Kelly's brings life to a standstill, like an old locomotive slamming to an unexpected stop. But slowly the train starts up again, even though you may not want it to. That's when I became truly conscious of just how much grief I possessed. A part of me wanted life to go on. Another part of me thought future happiness impossible. I defined grief as the process of learning to live again. I needed to learn to live without Kelly in my life.

Each day brought a new encounter, a new learning experience, a new grief. Some days I thought I was losing my mind. I tried to prepare myself for every possible emotion, tried to avoid certain painful situations, but suddenly I would find myself totally unprepared and invaded by cruel circumstances that rubbed my nose in the reality of Kelly's death.

As the days passed, there were brief moments when life seemed almost normal, such as one day at work. I was in my office working on an important project, feeling good about what I was doing. I enjoy my work, the satisfaction of setting goals and meeting them. I stopped momentarily to think and take a sip of coffee from my cup. I looked up and saw Kelly's blue eyes staring at me from the picture on my desk.

On another day, I was in my car listening to the radio, enjoying gospel music as I headed out of Minneapolis to meet a friend. Suddenly in front of me was the apartment building where Kelly lived. I pounded my fist on the dash of the car. My face turned red with rage. The music was drowned out by my shouts and screams. I was a wild man who had lost control. *Oh, God, when will life be happy again?*

One day it finally sank in: *Kelly is never coming back. I'm never going to see him on this earth again.* The thunder of grief echoed in my heart. I silently shouted my questions: *When does the aching go away? Will I ever be a functional person again? Does the pain ever subside?*

I wanted to talk about Kelly's death; and yet I wanted to avoid the subject completely. I wanted people to embrace me, hold me, cry with me; yet I wanted people to stay far away from me. I wanted people to know the great burden I was carrying, and I wanted people to believe that everything was perfectly fine in my life. A civil war was raging inside me, and the outcome was uncertain.

On a return flight to Minneapolis after a business trip to Suffolk, Virginia, a man near my age sat in the seat next to me. We exchanged the usual pleasantries.

"Hot day, huh?"

"You going home or leaving?"

"Are you on a business trip, or are you traveling for pleasure?"

Usually after you exchange such dialogue, you subconsciously conclude whether or not to take the conversation further and become more personal. On this particular day, with this particular gentleman, the conversation continued for a good part of the flight. We explained our respective businesses, talked about the general state of the economy and a little about politics. Eventually the conversation got around to family.

"I have four children who are all grown up and out on their own now." He took out his wallet and showed me a picture of his children. He was obviously proud, and I appreciated that. "How many kids do you have?" he asked.

I felt the color drain from my face. All the time he had been talking about his family, I was hoping he wouldn't ask me about mine. I was tired. The business trip had drained me. I had a long trip home. I had no energy and no desire to share Kelly's death with a stranger. *Why did he have to ask me, anyway? We just met. Why didn't he mind his own business?*

"How many kids do you have?" He had just asked the question, but it seemed like I waited an hour before responding.

"Two," I answered.

I was suddenly rocked by the turbulence of guilt. I had chosen not to include Kelly in my list of children, as though he had never lived. I mentally tried to justify my answer. *I'm sure the guy wanted to know how many living children I have,* I thought. *And besides, I don't really have to explain my son's death to a stranger. Talking about death is a real downer for most people, and there is no reason for me to make this surface conversation so heavy and depressing.* But all my attempts at justifying my lie didn't work. I had been untruthful. The truth was I had three children, and one of them was dead.

The man went on talking about his children, unconscious of the war raging inside me. I tried to figure out how I could bring the conversation back to the number of children I had and explain the truth.

I looked for opportunities to say, "Let me explain something. You asked me how many children I have and I told you two. Well, I had three but one died."

I thought the man would probably think it strange if I brought that up now. Most certainly he would say, "I'm sorry to hear that." And then he would ask, "How did he die?"

And I would say, "He took his own life." And a blanket of ice would descend from the plane's air vents and cover us with a chill.

Would he dare ask how? Would he dare ask why? Would I feel the need to explain the details of Kelly's death to this stranger whom I suddenly resented? But I knew it wasn't the stranger's fault. And certainly I did not need to be ashamed of Kelly's death—or did I? I told myself repeatedly that Kelly was responsible for his own death, the disease of depression driving him to the point where death seemed the only alternative. And yet, whenever I heard the words *death* and *suicide,* I was flooded with emotions I had not yet even identified.

I never did tell the man with four kids that I really had three, but as I entered the terminal and said good-bye to him, I vowed that I would never deny my son again.

A big part of the grief process, of learning to live again, is facing people and facing up to the reality of life without the one you love. Returning to work, I became consciously aware of how people treated me differently. Some seemed to avoid me, especially men. Conversations that did occur were often awkward.

"I was very sorry to hear about your son, Mr. Nygaard."

"Thank you very much," I would answer. Then there would often be a pregnant pause. What do you say next?

"I have been praying for you and your wife." Many people told Mary and me that we were in their prayers.

"Thanks. We really appreciate it," I would usually remark.

Some people would come up to me and ask, "How are you doing?"

The honest answer would have been "I don't know." Because I really didn't. What did I have to compare it with? I would usually answer, "I'm hanging in there and taking life one day at a time." Or I'd say, "I'm doing okay, but it is hard." Both answers were truthful, but I wondered if I could ever truly explain to anyone how I was really doing.

One day the telephone rang at our home. Mary answered it. It was the mother of one of Kelly's friends.

"My son wanted to come over to your house and tell you that he and his wife are expecting their first baby, but I told him not to."

"Why did you do that?" Mary asked.

"I was afraid that you would be too emotionally affected, and I didn't want him to hurt your feelings."

When Mary told me about the conversation, I got angry. "What's going on?" I asked. "Do we have signs around our necks that say STAY AWAY? Do we have leprosy?" I realized that the woman who called had our best interest at heart. She knew we could not help but think of how we would never know Kelly's children, and she was trying to save us the pain. What both Mary and I came to understand, however, is experiencing pain is part of the healing process. You can try to avoid the pain, but sooner or later you have to face it.

In his book *A Grief Observed,* C.S. Lewis makes the following statement concerning his grief: "An odd by-product of my loss is that I'm aware of being an embarrassment to everyone I meet. I see people, as they approach me, trying to make up their minds whether they'll say something about it or not. I hate it if they do, and if they don't." I knew exactly how Lewis felt.

One day at work an employee came up to me and asked, "How are you doing, Mr. Nygaard?"

I started to say, "Fine, thank you," but then I stopped. I looked the man in the eye, and I could tell that he was sincere. "Well, Joe," I said, "you know that my son Kelly took his own life a few months ago. Some days I don't feel like I have an ounce of energy."

"I can't begin to understand how painful that must be, but I can identify a little bit. You see, my son killed someone—he shot a man—and he has been convicted of murder. It looks like he might spend the rest of his life in prison."

We stood there for a moment, suddenly aware of each other's pain. I wondered how many others carried similar burdens. The bolder I became in sharing my circumstance, my pain, the more I discovered how the world is filled with people carrying truckloads of grief. My vulnerability allowed others to be vulnerable. In our openness, we could comfort and console one another. I was learning to strip off the mask of strength and expose the real me, as a child again, groping to find my way.

The more I shared, the less embarrassed I became. The process of sharing must begin at home. It starts by talking about what happened. We must create an atmosphere that says it's okay to cry, it's okay to laugh, it's okay to express whatever you feel, it's okay to ask whatever you want to ask, no matter how absurd the question might seem. It's okay. Home is where I learned that it was acceptable to be vulnerable. God then gave me the courage to share my vulnerability at work and elsewhere outside the home.

All of these factors contributed to our decision to attend *Survivors of Suicide,* as well as the *Compassionate Friends* group we later attended. The people in these groups gave us permission to experience and express our feelings, not just deny or suppress them. They could not only sympathize, but empathize.

One night as Mary and I attended a meeting of *Compassionate Friends,* a lady began to share.

"My oldest son, Pete, was killed in a plane

crash. I didn't think I could survive his death. My heart was broken. Every day was a painful reminder that life would never again be the same. I prayed for peace and comfort, but peace was elusive. And then my son Jimmy shot himself, and I realized that there was another valley of grief, even deeper and more painful than the first one."

Tears gently rolled down her face. Those seated on either side of her clutched her hands or placed their arms around her shoulders. No one gave advice. No one offered a quick fix. The words that were eventually spoken merely confirmed an understanding and acceptance of her pain.

"The hardest thing I had to come to grips with," said a man named Frank, "was my total inability to change the situation. All my life I had been in control. I was a master at control. I decided what the desired outcome was. I figured out what I needed to do to bring out the desired outcome, and I did it. After my son killed himself, I lost control. I knew what the desired outcome was: I wanted my son to be alive again. But it took me many months, almost a year, to realize that no matter what I tried to do, no matter how hard I worked, I could not bring my son back to life again."

Frank's words could have been mine. These people understood where I was in my pain, even though I wasn't totally certain myself. These people knew without my even trying to explain. Not only did they understand the depth of my pain, but they had survived their own. It was a small ray of sunshine in an otherwise dark and cloudy sky, but I was at least willing now to believe that I could survive, too.

"I thought the people in my church would offer the most support," said a younger lady. "But when my Krista took her life, some members in my church actually told me that it was impossible for someone who committed suicide to go to heaven."

Although no one had ever made such a comment to Mary or me, I knew there were those who believe that suicide is an unforgivable sin. They believe that since it is the last act a person commits, they are unable to repent of the sin; therefore, God cannot forgive them, and he condemns them to hell. Mary and I had to come to terms with what we believed about suicide and eternity. We knew that Kelly loved God and knew Jesus. When we cleaned out his apartment after his death, we found his Bible lying open on the night stand beside his bed. As we studied the Scriptures, we became more and more certain that Christ's blood forgives sin—past, present, and future. Kelly had accepted Christ's forgiveness and grace. Kelly died of an illness. I could not believe in a God who would turn away his own child who had suffered and died a painful death.

One night I had a dream. It is still very vivid to me. I was asking God the question that kept haunting me: *Why did you allow this to happen, God? Why?*

God's voice answered firmly and yet gently: "Don't you understand, Reuel? I didn't want Kelly here with me now. I had a wonderful life planned for him. But he is here, and I'm taking wonderful care of him."

I woke up trembling. "Mary," I said, shaking her shoulder. "Mary, did you hear him?"

"Hear what?" Groggily, she opened her eyes and squinted at me.

"Didn't you hear him? I could hear God talking to me as plainly as I'm talking to you. He told me that he didn't want Kelly in heaven yet, but since he is there, God is going to take wonderful care of him. I heard it as plain as day."

The tears Mary and I cried together that night were different. They were tears of gladness, knowing that the only one who could possibly love Kelly more than we could was faithfully watching over him.

I found much comfort from that dream, and from that night on I never doubted that Kelly was at home with the Lord.

It took me a few group meetings before I could share some of my feelings and experiences with others in our *Survivors of Suicide* and *Compassionate Friends* groups. But I learned that was acceptable, too. God was stripping me of my self-sufficiency. I was learning to lean—on him and on others.

One night as Mary and I were having devotions, a verse from Psalms jumped off the page at me.

"Cease striving and know that I am God" (Psalm 46:10 NASB). In the New International Version the same verse reads, "Be still, and know that I am God." I could hear God speaking to me as plainly as he did in my dream. "Be still, Reuel. I'm in charge. I'm in control. Let me take charge of all these circumstances in your life. You can't do it. I can. Let me."

Striving is what I had always been best at.

Although I had believed in God my entire life, I was now beginning to embark on a new journey of faith.

Chapter Seven

"Dear Kelly"

What we need to do is find out what the bullet did to you."

"That's what the counselor told me," Kent said. "I've been thinking a lot about it, and I realize that Kelly's bullet hit me, too."

I didn't comment immediately, but I knew that the counselor was right. The bullet from Kelly's gun had pierced all of our hearts. Grandmother Nygaard had been shot. The grandson she loved so much, the one who doted on her, had suddenly been taken from her, leaving a void in her old life that was impossible to fill. Kent and Scott and Sherry had been shot, and the bullet had forever closed a chapter in their lives. Dawn had been shot. Kelly's friends had been shot. And Mary and me?

Words can't express the damage the bullet did to us. Kelly's pain ended with his death. Ours didn't. Our pain only began.

All of us were learning that healing came slowly. I had heard of Elisabeth Kübler-Ross's "Five Stages of Death and Dying," and I realized that for many weeks and months I jumped from stage to stage. It was not an orderly progression. I would often take two steps forward and then three steps back. One day I would think I had broken through my denial and had reached whole-hearted acceptance of Kelly's death. Moments later I would find myself bargaining, denying that the tragedy had ever happened.

I still would not admit that I was angry. *How could I be angry at Kelly? Poor Kelly! The pain and the loss he'd experienced! I should be ashamed of myself to even consider being angry with him! Being angry at Kelly is a betrayal of my son. I'm not angry.*

As Mary and I attended more support group meetings, I learned that my feelings, although very personal, were not unique. Others who had survived tragedies had similar feelings. They, too, had vacillated between denial and acceptance. They, too, denied their anger.

One night at a support group meeting, a young mother spoke. "I've finally had to admit that I'm angry because my daughter killed herself," she said. "Only since I've admitted it am I really able to forgive her and get on with my life."

I thought about what she had said and did a little self-evaluation. Was I angry at Kelly? Did I need to forgive him? I felt guilty even asking myself the questions.

Months later, when Kent shared his counselor's comment, I wondered, *Just what did the bullet do to me?* I realized that the bullet had ripped through my soul and my mind and had wreaked havoc on my life.

I had been shot full of shame. Although I knew I was not responsible for Kelly's death, a part of me whispered: *You were a failure as a father.* "No, I was not!" I would scream back, and although I know I was a good father, the whispering in my soul was forever disconcerting.

You should have been aware that he was severely depressed. You blew it! This taunt was louder. Guilt joined its cousin shame in this taunt again and again, and I was less adamant in defending myself. In fact, my heart echoed their sentiments: "You're right. If only I had known more about the disease of depression, I could have done more to get Kelly some help."

Many times I stared at the list of questions asked of people to determine if they are suffering from depression: Do you feel sad most of the time? Do you feel you have little to look forward to in life? Do you feel that you are bad or worthless? Do your moods swing from highs to lows? Have you lost interest in the activities of everyday life? Do you have frequent crying spells? Have you pulled away emotionally from family and friends? Do you have thoughts about suicide? Do you have trouble meeting your work responsibilities? Do you find it easier to sleep than stay awake? Have you recently lost a person who is close to you? And the list went on. (A more complete list of symptoms is listed in the epilogue.)

The pamphlet in which I had first read the list had said that if a person answered yes to even a few of the questions, he or she might be suffering from depression and should seriously consider seeing a counselor. I studied the list. I guessed Kelly could have answered yes to over two-thirds of the questions. *Why hadn't I noticed? Why?*

Yes, the bullet had shot me with shame and guilt, with intense pain I felt that was almost impossible to endure. As I studied the list of depressive symptoms, I realized that I was suffering from depression. I continued to experience mood swings that came about more suddenly than that summer storm our family had endured on the banks of Lake Superior when Kelly was just a baby. I was sad more often than not, and I found myself experiencing frequent crying spells. Always an early riser, I was now waking up even earlier and finding it almost impossible to go back to sleep. I had lost much of the excitement I used to have for running and physical exercise. Although everything was in place to fulfill our dream of constructing a log cabin on the banks of North Long Lake, I found myself devoid of enthusiasm for the project and feeling almost guilty about going on with life without Kelly.

Mary experienced many of the same signs of depression that I did, and although our support groups were helpful, we felt we needed more intense help. "I think we should see a grief counselor," Mary said. And I agreed. We made an appointment and, of course, we were somewhat apprehensive about it. Others assured us that going to a counselor was the right thing to do. Some people think that going to a counselor, a psychologist, or a psychiatrist is a sign of weakness. One senator's bid for vice-president was sabotaged because it was disclosed that he had visited a psychiatrist. Many people felt: "We can't have a vice-president, the man who is one heartbeat away from the chief office in our country, who sees a shrink!" Although that happened in the late 1960s, the attitude is still prevalent among some people today. It is a damaging attitude that keeps many people from receiving invaluable help. No, seeing a counselor is not a sign of weakness, but rather a sign of strength. The truly strong admit their weaknesses.

Mary and I went to see the counselor, and he helped us recognize feelings that we were unaware of. He helped us face the issues head-on, break denial, and move closer to acceptance. Without his help, the process would have taken much longer, we believe. We would have slowly staggered forward and perhaps never identified some of our true feelings.

Such as anger.

As my denial broke more completely, I finally admitted it: I was angry at Kelly. He deprived us of his love. He stole from us one of the greatest joys of our lives. He robbed us of years of building memories, sharing dreams, and fulfilling our hopes. He had been selfish. He had thought only of himself. And although I knew that this was the nature of the disease of depression, I was still angry. I had come to grips with the circumstances that led to Kelly's death. I understood the hideous disease of depression. I knew that Kelly was not thinking rationally. Nonetheless, his actions had hurt me deeply. He had shot me, too. And just as his depression was understandable, so was my anger, and I did not have to be ashamed of it. It was not a betrayal of my son.

"Unless you admit your anger and forgive Kelly," the counselor said, "the anger will go underground and adversely affect the healing process."

I was somewhat startled to think that I had to forgive Kelly. I still had a hard time admitting that I was angry with him. I tried so hard to see only the good in him that it was difficult to admit his faults. I wrestled again with those feelings of betrayal.

"If we work at only seeing the good and picture our departed loved one as being without fault, we are deceiving ourselves," the counselor said. "Kelly committed suicide. It was *not* a good thing to do. Because of his depression, we can understand why he did it, but regardless, it was not a good thing to do. It has caused a tremendous amount of pain in many lives. Some lives will never be the same again. Admit it. He made the worst decision possible, a decision that totally turned your life upside down. You have a reason to be angry."

I felt anger rise up inside me. I thought I was angry at the counselor for saying that Kelly had made a bad decision, but then I realized that I was really angry because of Kelly's decision, not the counselor's comment.

I have since learned that even in natural deaths those left behind often experience anger. They feel deserted, and who is to blame? The one that deserted them. Or God. I didn't think I was angry at God. That was a feeling I had not yet identified, but I had finally realized that I was angry at Kelly.

Feelings of anger are complicated, not easily recognizable, and are often mistaken for other feelings. A friend of mine was sharing the circumstances of a painful divorce he was going through. "I love my wife so much," he said. "I can't believe she is doing what she is doing."

We talked a bit more, and then I said, "You are really angry at your wife, aren't you?"

"I am not," he shot back, with rage in his eyes.

"After I admitted my anger concerning Kelly's death," I told my friend, "I learned from my counseling that anger manifests itself in a number of different feelings. Individuals may not realize that they are angry, but they feel as though they have been deliberately abandoned. They may feel that their own self-worth has been challenged. They may actually inherit some of the pain and confusion of their loved one who abandoned them. They often feel the need to try to explain to the world the circumstances of what has happened and to make sense of it all. In the end, their belief in their loved one is often tarnished, although they may feel ashamed to admit it. These feelings are all closely related to anger.

"Do you have any of those feelings?" I asked.

There was a moment's silence. He looked as if he were in shock. "I've experienced them all," he finally answered.

My friend and I talked some more about anger, and it seemed almost like a relief for him to admit that, yes, he was angry at his wife for abandoning him. He realized too, just as I did with Kelly, that being angry at someone does not change your love for him or her.

This friend, struggling through the pain of divorce, was only one of the many that God was going to send into my life, although I wasn't aware of it at the time. "Someone told me that depression often results from anger that is stuffed down inside," I said. "Depression is often anger turned inward. We need to admit our anger and choose to forgive. It is perhaps the most important part of the healing process."

I felt like the blind leading the blind, but I realized that the counseling Mary and I were receiving was our seeing-eye dog. I discovered joy in sharing my dog—my discoveries—with others who were groping in the darkness.

You have to find out what the bullet did to you. I kept hearing those words of Kent's counselor. "It might be very helpful for you to visit Kelly's grave and express your feelings to him," my counselor recommended. "Some people talk to a picture of the one who has committed suicide or has died, and some write a letter. Reuel, I recommend that you express your feelings to Kelly in one of these ways."

I thought about my options. Writing down my thoughts in a letter seemed the best way of making sure I expressed everything I wanted and needed to say. I sat at my desk, pen in hand, thinking about writing this letter to Kelly that I knew he would never read. Was this a lesson in futility? *No,* I quickly concluded. This letter was as important as the letter I wrote to Kelly that night in my hotel room as he was about to graduate from high school. In many ways, it was more important.

"Dear Kelly," I wrote, and the tears came uncontrollably. With the tears came a multitude of other emotions I could identify now: anger, grief, confusion, fear, loneliness, abandonment, denial, acceptance, and, most importantly, love and forgiveness.

I saw so much promise and potential in your life, Kelly. Obviously, you didn't. I saw so many reasons you had to live. Obviously, you didn't. You never gave me the opportunity to help you out. I'm angry, Kelly. I'm angry. Why didn't you know that I would have done anything to help you? Do you realize the pain that you have caused your mother, your brothers, your friends, your relatives? Do you realize how much pain we feel? Do you realize, Kelly, how unfair you've been to us? Oh, Kelly, why didn't you give me a chance to help you?

You made the worst of all possible decisions, Kelly. And yet, I'm not having as much difficulty understanding the decision you made as I am in bearing the pain. I understand your depression, Kelly, and why you did what you did, but I'm having a very difficult time handling my own pain. You hurt me deeply, Kelly.

Had I been too harsh? I reread what I had written. No. It was how I felt. Suddenly I felt a release in my spirit. This catharsis had freed me of something, had exposed the truth, and the truth felt very liberating.

But I love you, Kelly, my son. I love you.

And I forgive you. I choose not to hold this against you. I will always love you and will look forward to that day when we will be together again.

I ended this letter just as I had the letter from New York:

I Love You, Kelly,
Dad

Chapter Eight

Passages

The investigator laid the file before us on the conference table in the sheriff's office. "Here it is," he said with an air of resignation. "I'll try to answer any questions that you have."

This man had investigated Kelly's death. He had gone to Dawn's home. He had written the report. He had concluded that it was a suicide. "My wife and I would like to see a copy of your investigation," I said when I had first called him.

"Mr. Nygaard," the investigator had answered with genuine kindness in his voice, "I wouldn't recommend it. The report could be very painful for you. It would be best for you not to pursue the matter any further. Your son is dead. He committed suicide."

"My wife and I must see the records. We still

have some questions that need answers."

"It is not a good idea, Mr. Nygaard."

"We want to see his file. When can we see it?"

The investigator realized that we would not be deterred. "You can come to the office any time."

Later that afternoon we sat in the sheriff's conference room with the file before us. It was just another manila file among many in the sheriff's filing cabinets, but this file bore the name *Kelly Jon Nygaard,* and the conclusion: *Suicide. Self-inflicted gunshot wound to the chest. March 1, 1988.* This file was different from the other files. This file contained all the investigator had discovered about the final minutes of our son's life, and we wanted to know—we had to know—whatever there was to know.

I don't know what we expected to find, but a part of me still doubted that Kelly had committed suicide. I had wondered if perhaps he had been murdered. Stranger things had happened. Was it possible that this file would contain some information that would offer a more acceptable explanation of Kelly's death?

Apprehensively, we opened the file. Together Mary and I read all of the investigator's notes. The investigation had been very complete. The investigator had even found the gas station where Kelly had purchased the shells for the rifle. The clerk remembered selling the shells to him. The investigator had reconstructed Kelly's last few hours. Kelly had gone from school to the gas station to buy the bullets, then to Dawn's house—where he removed one of her father's guns from the gun case, crawled into Dawn's bed, put the gun to his chest, and shot himself through the heart. One shot. The coroner's report concluded that death had been immediate.

"Why did it take so long to get an ambulance?" We asked the question even though we knew that an ambulance would have done no good.

"Why weren't we notified sooner?" Again we asked, although we knew the answer: it took time to contact the chaplain and send him to our home.

"How long after Kelly shot himself was his body discovered?"

"Why didn't the neighbors hear the shot?"

The investigator patiently answered our questions, conscious of our pain, aware of our need to understand, our need to know all the details, no matter how painful.

"I guess this was a necessary part of our healing process," I said as we rose to leave.

"I understand, Mr. and Mrs. Nygaard. I'm very sorry. I really am."

Mary and I left the sheriff's office without a doubt in our minds that Kelly had committed suicide. Although a new wave of pain crashed in upon us, we had made another passage in our journey of recovery.

Mary and I have made many passages, and we continue to do so. Each day offers some new bridge to recovery. This book, in large part, is another bridge in our journey. Recently we spent time talking with our neighbor, Peggy, who was with Mary after she learned that Kelly had died. Peggy recalled many details of those hours that had been a blank in Mary's mind. Both Mary and I have discovered that we cannot deny our curiosity to know all the details concerning Kelly's death and the events surrounding his death. I liken our curiosity to the cancer patient who wants to know the truth concerning his cancer. Not knowing is worse than the truth.

We both continued our counseling, and I reaffirmed my definition of grief as "learning to live again." I think it is an appropriate definition. Given this definition, grief is not an enemy, but rather an essential, unavoidable part of life—a friend who understands the pain, encourages you to face the truth, and gently prods you to go on with your journey, to go on with life. No, grief is not an enemy, and neither is death. Death is as essential a part of living as birth. Only through death can we experience the ultimate of Christ's love for us. A tragic loss in one's life—whether it be through suicide, death by illness, divorce or separation, or loss of a job or financial status—is a passage that will either result in a loss of faith or a discovery of faith.

I had been to many funerals in my life, funerals of close friends and relatives, but I had never seen this side of death before. I had heard preachers speak of the brevity of life, and I had heard them preach the promises of eternal life to those who believe. Although I had built my life and my faith on the certainty of those words, experience was now the greatest teacher.

Someone said, "A death like Kelly's is enough to make a guy lose his faith."

"No," I said, "it is enough to make a guy use his faith."

The words of Proverbs 24:10 came to my mind: "If you are slack in the day of distress, your strength is limited." These had been days of distress, no doubt about it, but they were also days when God was teaching me to lean on him, to surrender, to "cease striving." *Let God be God. Put your faith in him.* Those words came to me again and again. Consciously I decided, *I'm not going to* lose *my faith. I'm going to* use *my faith.*

This was a significant decision. The truth of Scripture presented itself to me in a new way. I read these verses from James with a new understanding and appreciation:

> *Look here, you people who say, "Today or tomorrow we are going to such and such a town, stay there a year, and open up a profitable business."*
>
> *How do you know what is going to happen tomorrow? For the length of your lives is as uncertain as the morning fog—now you see it; soon it is gone. (James 4:13-14)*

Life is a vapor. Kelly had lived only twenty-three years on this earth, but even those who live to be a hundred feel that life passes quickly. As I approach sixty, I can't believe that it has all gone by so fast. I already qualify for the senior citizen's discount at restaurants. Many people my age have already retired. But it was just yesterday I was sliding down Charlie's Hill. Just yesterday I set the high school pole vault record and ran the Boston Marathon. It was just yesterday I took Mary's hand in marriage, slipped the ring on her finger, and pledged myself to her until death do us part. It was just yesterday, wasn't it, that our first son was born?

No. The years pass quickly. We make many passages and cross many rivers. Some rivers have no bridges, and crossing is only possible in the boat called *faith*.

"Is joy really possible again?" I asked my Lord.

"Get in the boat," was all that Jesus said.

Chapter Nine

Turning Tragedy into Triumph

Reuel, do you believe in free speech?" a friend of mine asked on the phone one day.

"Of course I do," I answered automatically.

"Then how about coming and giving one to Bible Study Fellowship?"

I had heard the line before and couldn't believe I had fallen for it.

"Well, what would I talk about?"

"That's up to you and God, Reuel; why don't you pray about it? We'd like for you to share."

Share what? I wondered. There were over two hundred men in our BSF group, and I knew they all knew about Kelly. If I stood before them to talk about my faith in Christ, the source of comfort I found in the Scriptures, how could I do it without talking about Kelly? Would I pretend that nothing had happened and select another topic? Or could I possibly share my grief? Was I ready to talk about it? Wasn't there too much raw pain? Opening up to a grief counselor or a support group was one thing; but sharing in front of two hundred professional men, so seemingly secure and "all together," was quite another. And yet I knew that beneath the masks of control were people who had suffered just like me. *Compassionate Friends* and *Survivors of Suicide* had opened my eyes to the fact that people go through each day deeply in pain, but holding it all inside.

At Kelly's funeral, John Vawter had read a paragraph from a letter written by a couple who were in pain, who were experiencing their deepest time of hurting. They compared it to being in a hospital intensive care unit. "We thought of how much caring would take place if we were physically in critical condition," they wrote. "There would be phone calls, many prayers, meals brought to our home, and concerned tears. But it's quiet and lonely when your spirit is crushed and your heart is broken. On the outside people view you as though you're just fine and are perhaps even envious of your situation."

I could identify. My spirit had been crushed and my heart broken. I had been on that same critical list. But I went to church each Sunday. I went to work each day. To those in my corporation, I was "the vice-president" and I had "made it."

We often wear masks to hide our pain. Recently I read a poem by Paul Laurence Dunbar, "We Wear the Mask."

We wear the mask that grins and lies,
It hides our cheeks and shades our eyes—
This debt we pay to human guile;
With torn and bleeding hearts we smile,
And mouth with myriad subtleties.

Why should the world be otherwise,
In counting all our tears and sighs?
Nay, let them only see us, while
We wear the mask.

We smile, but, O great Christ, our cries
To thee from tortured souls arise.
We sing, but oh the clay is vile
Beneath our feet, and long the mile;
But let the world dream otherwise,
We wear the mask.

Many of the men in our Bible Study Fellowship group were well-respected and revered in the Minneapolis area. They were corporate executives, highly successful businessmen, famous personalities. Could it be possible that some of them were on God's critical list? Did any of them wear a mask? I was reminded of the famous poem "Richard Cory" by Edwin Arlington

Robinson. Richard Cory was the envy of the town. He was a handsome gentleman who had it all.

And he was rich—yes, richer than a king—
And admirably schooled in every grace;
In fine, we thought that he was everything
To make us wish that we were in his place.

But there was more to Richard Cory than met the eye—and no one looked beyond the mask of success.

So on we worked, and waited for the light,
And went without the meat, and cursed the bread;
And Richard Cory, one calm summer night,
Went home and put a bullet through his head.

As I considered the invitation to speak, I thought of Richard Cory—and, of course, of Kelly. I wondered if another Richard Cory or another Kelly might attend that meeting. If even one man out of two hundred could gain hope from what I could share, then it was definitely worth the risk.

I felt God tugging on my heart, and I accepted the invitation. "I want to talk about Kelly and what his death has done to my faith."

"I'm sure that'll be tough for you, Reuel," my friend answered, "but it will reach a lot of people. All of us have wondered why bad things happen to good people. You have survived one of the worst things that can happen to a parent. If you can still talk about *faith*...well, then, I think we can learn a great deal from you."

"I don't have any answers. All I can do is share what I've learned."

"That's all we ask, Reuel."

After I hung up the phone, I felt a strange ambivalence. I was excited about the opportunity to talk about Kelly's suicide. If our experiences could in some way help someone else, then Kelly's death would not be completely in vain. If my vulnerability allowed someone else to be vulnerable, too, then my pain would not have been in vain. And yet, I was scared stiff.

At Kelly's funeral Pastor Vawter had issued a challenge to Mary and me. We had reread it a number of times: "Reuel and Mary, you can take the next twenty or thirty years and spend it hiding at your cabin, or you can turn this tragedy into triumph. I would just ask you to recall that Mothers Against Drunk Drivers is making a difference in our society today because, when a young mother's child was killed by a drunk driver, she decided to make a difference and turn her tragedy into triumph."

I had often wondered how I could possibly turn

Kelly's death into a triumph. God seemed to be telling me: *Share your pain, share your story, share your faith.* And now with this opportunity to speak to BSF, God was opening a door.

I reread the rest of John Vawter's words: "Reuel and Mary, you are a unique couple. Your intellect, your spiritual depth, your personalities, your warmth. And I believe that if you would somehow seek God in a new way, even having suffered the pain of losing your son to suicide, that God will use the depth that He's built into your lives over the years, and use the gifts that He has given to you to affect thousands of lives. Let God build a triumph out of this tragedy. I think God has something special for you."

I realized that this was another passage, another turning point. God was saying, *The time of self-absorption is past; it is time to reach out to others.*

I was ready. But what was I going to *say?*

❖ ❖

"God comforts us in our affliction so that we might comfort others in theirs." More of Pastor Vawter's funeral words. I turned to them again as I thought about my upcoming talk to the Bible Study Fellowship Group. I turned to the scripture reference that John had cited, 2 Corinthians 1, and I read Paul's words again:

> *Grace to you and peace from God our Father and the Lord Jesus Christ.*

Blessed be the God and Father of our Lord Jesus Christ, the Father of mercies and God of all comfort; who comforts us in all our affliction so that we may be able to comfort those who are in any affliction with the comfort with which we ourselves are comforted by God.

For just as the sufferings of Christ are ours in abundance, so also our comfort is abundant through Christ.

But if we are afflicted, it is for your comfort and salvation; or if we are comforted, it is for your comfort, which is effective in the patient enduring of the same sufferings which we also suffer; and our hope for you is firmly grounded, knowing that as you are sharers of our sufferings, so also you are sharers of our comfort.

For we do not want you to be unaware, brethren, of our affliction which came to us in Asia, that we were burdened excessively, beyond our strength, so that we despaired even of life; indeed, we had the sentence of death within ourselves in order that we should not trust in ourselves, but in God who raises the dead; who delivered us from so great a peril of death, and will deliver us, he on whom we have set our hope. And he will yet deliver us, you also joining in helping us through your prayers, that thanks may be given by many persons on our behalf for the favor bestowed upon us through the prayers of many. (2 Corinthians 1:2-11)

I studied this Scripture again and again. Amazing. Paul understood hardship and suffering. In fact, at the moment of Paul's conversion on the Damascus road, God made a promise to Ananias concerning Paul: "I will show him how much he must suffer for my name's sake" (Acts 9:16). Paul's suffering began immediately and lasted for over thirty years. He was put in stocks, imprisoned for years at a time, beaten repeatedly, stoned, shipwrecked, and ultimately beheaded by a Roman blade.

Paul understood suffering, and yet look at this:

> *And the crowd rose up together against them [Paul and Silas] and the chief magistrates tore their robes off them, and proceeded to order them to be beaten with rods.*
>
> *And when they had inflicted many blows upon them, they threw them into prison, commanding the jailer to guard them securely; and he, having received such a command, threw them into the inner prison, and fastened their feet in the stocks,*
>
> *But about midnight Paul and Silas were praying and singing hymns of praise to God, and the prisoners were listening to them. (Acts 16:22-25)*

Paul sang in prison! He'd been beaten with a rod, shackled, and thrown into the deepest, darkest

Roman dungeon—and yet he sang! What a testimony. Could I sing despite my suffering?

I read 2 Corinthians 1:3,4 from the Living Bible paraphrase:

> *What a wonderful God we have—he is the Father of our Lord Jesus Christ, the source of every mercy, and the one who so wonderfully comforts and strengthens us in our hardships and trials. And why does he do this? So that when others are troubled, needing our sympathy and encouragement, we can pass on to them this same help and comfort God has given us.*

The Word does not say that God's comfort will cause the suffering to go away. Being a Christian doesn't mean our hardships will all disappear. God is not responsible for making Christ's followers healthy and rich, but God has promised that he can and will transform our suffering into glory. He does not necessarily remove the suffering from us, but he does transform it.

I looked closely at verse 5. In the Living Bible it reads: "You can be sure that the more we undergo sufferings for Christ, the more he will shower us with his comfort and encouragement." I was becoming more and more conscious of how my suffering was the opportunity God was giving me to minister.

I thought of a friend of mine who is a recovering

alcoholic. He told me about the value of his twelve - step group. "These folks understand," he said. "They've been where I am. I can't tell you', Reuel, how much that means."

Mary and I met many people who were sympathetic to our situation, who tried to appreciate and understand our grief. But when a lady looked at us at a support group meeting and said, "My son shot himself, too," we knew that she truly understood. God was showing me that he could use my pain to comfort others with similar pain.

About two months after Kelly's suicide, a neighbor called to tell us that another neighbor's teenage daughter had asphyxiated herself by carbon monoxide poisoning. Although we didn't know the family very well, we did know that God told us to go visit them. We went to their home the evening after the funeral. We didn't go sooner because we knew from our own experience that the first few days are spent in shock. After the funeral, however, most people think that life is supposed to "get back to normal"—and yet it is the time when the survivors realize that life will never quite be "normal" again.

When we went to our neighbor's home, we didn't know exactly what we were going to say, but Mary and I both knew that we could be a comfort to others who suffer because we had suffered, too. We were willing to try to be that comfort.

I've learned that at times hugs work better than words, and at first, that's what we did; we embraced as they opened the door to their home. Our neighbors invited us in, and within moments they were sharing their feelings, obviously grateful that we understood. We shared our experience with Kelly—not so much the details of his death, but the details of our recovery: the importance of support, facing the issues head-on, and discovering the full measure of God's love. Our mere presence was a signal to these folks that survival is possible, and we knew from our own experience how much they needed to know that.

That night was another passage, another river crossed in the boat called *faith.* We received comfort from giving comfort, and this helped heal a part of the hurt we felt.

Since that night there have been many opportunities to reach out to others who have lost a child or a loved one through suicide. But Mary and I have not limited ourselves to survivors of suicide because, although suicide definitely involves a different type of pain, we know that the pain is similar for anyone who experiences the death of a loved one. Each time we reach out to comfort, we receive comfort. Both of us prayed for opportunities to be this source of comfort for others. We know that it is the ministry God has called us to in the days we have left here, and we both desire to be faithful to this call upon our lives.

The opportunity to speak at BSF was a part of the new ministry to which God had called me. Now

I knew at least one thing I'd share with the guys: "God has not promised us a life without suffering, but he has promised to comfort us. And as he comforts us in our suffering, we can be a comfort to others."

❖ ❖

I looked at this first point of my talk. It made sense, but what else did I have to say? I studied Paul's words further: "We were burdened excessively, beyond our strength, so that we despaired even of life; indeed, we had the sentence of death within ourselves in order that we should not trust in ourselves, but in God who raises the dead" (2 Corinthians 1:8,9).

I had just found my second point: "We should not trust in ourselves, but in God." What had all of Paul's suffering taught him? "Lean on God. Trust him. You can't raise anybody from the dead, but God can. Only God can. Don't trust in yourself, Paul, trust in God!" God was now teaching me the same the thing, but it was very difficult for an independent person like me. My belief that "God helps those who help themselves" was wrong. God helps those who realize that without his help they are helpless. And truly we are. Only God can raise people from the dead!

I once heard a story about a man who decided to learn to walk a tightrope. He strung a rope in his backyard and practiced each day for many hours. His neighbor watched intently as the man fell repeatedly into the net below, only to get up and try again. As the days passed, the neighbor noticed that his tightrope-walking friend was becoming quite accomplished. Then one day the neighbor noticed that his friend was walking without a net. "Good work!" he yelled to man on the rope, who was now confident enough to wave back.

As the days and weeks of practice continued, the neighbor noticed how his friend kept raising the tightrope and extending the distance from pole to pole. He was amazed at how far his friend had progressed. Then one day he saw the man standing on the platform with a wheelbarrow. "What are you going to do?" he called to him.

"I am going to walk the tightrope pushing the wheelbarrow in front of me!" the daredevil answered back. "Do you think that I can do it?" he asked the neighbor.

"I'm sure you can! I've been watching you for weeks now. You are wonderful! I have complete faith in you!"

"Glad to hear it," said the man. "Will you come and get in the wheelbarrow?"

The neighbor, of course, refused. The story is an analogy of our Christian faith. We have witnessed the might and awesomeness of God. We've sung "How Great Thou Art" a thousand times and have acknowledged the power and the majesty of the God who is big enough to rule the universe and yet intimate enough to live within each heart. Like the watchful neighbor, we have shouted, "I have complete faith in you!" But then God says, "Come, get into my wheelbarrow." And we refuse.

Several years ago I heard a well-known preacher explain the time in his life when he first realized that he was powerless, that his fate lay totally in the hands of God. He was a passenger on a plane, and as the plane began to land the pilot informed the passengers that he was uncertain if the landing gear had locked in place. All the passengers were forced to prepare for a crash landing. The pastor, who was afraid of flying to begin with, was now paralyzed with fear. There was absolutely nothing he could do. It wouldn't help to yell at the pilot or the flight attendants. He could blame anyone and everyone, but passing blame would not solve a thing. Then he realized there was really only one thing he could do: trust God. He did, and the plane landed safely, the landing gear securely locked in place.

My experience has been that many of us do not surrender complete control until we have no other options left. When we do surrender, give up and give in to God, we wonder why we didn't get in the wheelbarrow sooner.

Paul says that he "was burdened excessively." I could identify. He said he was "beyond strength." I knew what it felt like not to have any strength left. He said, "We despaired even of life." So what did Paul do? "We had this sentence of death within ourselves in order that we should not trust in ourselves, but in God." Paul learned not to trust in himself. His strength gave out. The burdens became too great. But God could carry the burdens. God could impart his strength.

This was the lesson that I had learned, too. "Get in the wheelbarrow, Reuel."

❖ ❖

As I studied 2 Corinthians 1:3-11, I took a piece of paper and wrote across the top: God allows suffering so...

v. 4—that we might be a comfort to others

v. 9—that we might totally trust in him

I understood those two reasons; I had even witnessed the application of them in my life. But as I looked at verse eleven, I got angry:

v. 11—that thanks may be given

I was willing to comfort others. I realized my need to trust God completely. But how could I possibly be thankful for what Kelly had done? The thought was absurd! I read the Scripture over and over. It listed a cross reference, so I turned to it. Another of Paul's letters said:

> *Rejoice in the Lord always; again I will say, rejoice!*
>
> *Let your forbearing spirit be known to all men. The Lord is near.*
>
> *Be anxious for nothing, but in everything by prayer and supplication with thanksgiving let your requests be made known to God.*

> *And the peace of God, which surpasses all comprehension, shall guard your hearts and your minds in Christ Jesus.*
>
> *Finally, brethren, whatever is true, whatever is honorable, whatever is right, whatever is pure, whatever is lovely, whatever is of good repute, if there is any excellence and if anything worthy of praise, let your mind dwell on these things.(Philippians 4:4-8)*

There it was again: "*In everything with thanksgiving.*" Surely, that couldn't mean the suicide of your son!

I turned to another cross reference and read some more: "Rejoice always; pray without ceasing; in everything give thanks; for this is God's will for you in Christ Jesus"(1 Thessalonians 5:16-18).

Rejoice *always?* In *everything* give thanks? Come on! It was like Romans 8:28, which many people loved to share with me: "And we know that God causes all things to work together for good to those who love God, to those who are called according to his purpose." I knew the verse well, but I doubted it. How was Kelly's death going to work out for good? And how was I supposed to thank God for this devastating tragedy in my life?

Well, I had my third point for my talk to the BSF group, but I wasn't sure I believed it. Could I fake it? Could I fake being thankful? I got down on my knees and poured out the contents of my heart to God, still unwilling, perhaps still unaware of the anger I harbored toward him. "God," I prayed, "I want to give thanks for Kelly's death, but I can't."

I sensed God's answer: "You are being honest, Reuel—with yourself and with me. This truth will set you free. Continue to trust in me, and you'll be able to offer thanks even in this situation."

God was able to use me to minister despite my doubt, I realized. In fact, my doubt seemed to motivate me to go deeper, to get closer to God. One theologian said that doubt is "the ants in the pants of faith," and I certainly understood that now. Although I doubted the possibility of thanking God for Kelly's suicide, I was willing to trust him nonetheless.

In the meantime, God continued to open more doors for Mary and me to help others. One day at work a young girl came into my office. "Can I talk to you for a minute, Mr. Nygaard?"

"Sure, come on in." I looked at the young woman, grief written on her face, and I understood her pain. "How are you doing?" I asked.

"Some days it is really hard." This mother's three-month-old daughter had died of Sudden Infant Death Syndrome. She wouldn't be able to look back on years of fond memories like I could with Kelly. But we had a common denominator: we were both members of that fraternity of parents who had survived the death of a child. As we visited, I realized that I was thankful that I could understand her pain and offer her sincere comfort. I felt a certain satisfaction knowing that God had used me in a way I could never have been used before.

Mary was flying home from a trip to San Francisco when the lady sitting next to her started talking about her family. "My son was killed by a drunk driver," she said. "I have a lot of issues that are still unresolved." Mary was able to take the woman's hand and say, "My twenty-three-year-old son took his own life; I understand unresolved issues."

The more we shared, the more we were thankful that God had given us this opportunity for ministry. The more we comforted others, the more comfort we received. The more pain we encountered, the more we realized how pain and suffering draw us to God in a new and intimate way. The truth of James's words became clearer to me each day:

> *When all kinds of trials and temptations crowd into your lives, my brothers, don't resent them as intruders, but welcome them as friends! Realize that they come to test your faith and to produce in you the quality of endurance. But let the process go on until that endurance is fully developed, and you will find you have become men of mature charter with the right sort of independence. (James 1:2-5; J.B. Phillips)*

Pain and suffering aren't intruders; they are friends. They have caused me to surrender my own self-sufficiency. They have taught me to lean completely on God. They are helping me grow in my faith as I learn that God's grace is sufficient. And I have to admit it—for this I *am* thankful. I have discovered that God is even greater than I thought he was.

One day as I was praying, I had a revelation. *God is a part of our fraternity, too. He not only lost his son, he* sacrificed *his son. God gave his son to die, and he did so for me, so that I could have eternal life. Yet so many people take his sacrifice for granted! How must that make God feel? My son died from a brain disease that caused him to take his life. What if I had been asked to sacrifice my son? Could I have placed Kelly on an altar as Abraham did with Isaac, as God did with Christ? That would have been more difficult than a suicide. Yes, God was a part of the same fraternity. And he understands.*

The day finally arrived for my talk to the BSF. Mary and I had prayed that God would use me and my vulnerability to touch lives for him. I have to admit I was more than a little anxious as I stood to speak. "I'd like to offer you just a glimpse into the life of Reuel Nygaard," I began.

I told them about Vernon Center and Charlie's Hill, about a young woman named Mary. I told them of three wonderful sons: Scott, Kent, and Kelly. I shared about my success in business, my rise up the corporate ladder, my servant-leadership philosophy of management. "I was living the American Dream," I said. "And then one day the American

Dream became a nightmare."

And then I told them about Kelly.

"Why?" I asked them, and I knew from the looks in their eyes and the spirit in the room that many of them had asked the same question.

I enjoyed sharing the three "so that" answers from 2 Corinthians 1, and when I shared the A,B,C's of faith, just as Pastor Vawter had done at Kelly's funeral, I was thankful that God had given me this opportunity to minister.

But I still wasn't thankful that Kelly was dead.

CHAPTER TEN

GOD SENT SOME ANGELS

For the first time in my life, I was indifferent about the approaching summer.

Usually I look forward to each new season, knowing that each season offers different opportunities, its own special invitation to enjoy life. Minnesota has four very distinct seasons, although some people joke that winter lasts for most of the year and the other three seasons last a week each. I've never found Minnesota winters to be as bad as some people make them out to be. Our family has always embraced winter; we enjoy downhill and cross country skiing, hockey, and ice fishing. Once the leaves are off the trees, I actually look forward to getting out my flannel shirt and my down-filled ski jacket. There's a new freshness in the air, and although it may freeze the tip of your nose, it sure is invigorating!

I always get a kick out of explaining the love Minnesotans have for ice fishing to my friends from the south. They find it impossible to believe that our 10,000 lakes freeze, and we use them as highways to transport us to the fish houses we build on the ice.

"You mean you actually drive on the lakes in your cars? How thick does the ice get?" they ask incredulously.

"Oh, most places it is three to five feet thick. Some fish houses have three stories!"

"You're kidding!"

"No. Some Minnesotans live in their fish houses all winter, sleep in 'em, you know."

At this point, our friends begin to suspect that we are elaborating on reality a bit for the sake of the joke, but they're still not quite sure how to respond.

"Are you serious?"

"Ya, sure, you betcha," I answer in my best Norwegian accent. "Dis is Minnesota, you know."

But come March I'm usually ready for the ice to leave the lakes, eager for warmer days, green leaves, the smell of new grass, a robin's return song. Then I welcome the summer sun which will put a little color back into my faded face.

But this summer would be different. It would be the first summer without Kelly.

I heard someone say that the greatest distance in the world is the eighteen inches between the head and the heart. In my head I knew that Kelly was with Jesus, and Jesus was taking good care of my son. I knew that God was using my suffering as an opportunity to minister and reach out to others who suffered, too. I had even had the opportunity to do a television show and share about depression, a disease I discovered few people really understood. I knew, too, that God had used the suffering in my life to teach me to lean completely on him, to give up and give in to his will. I knew all this in my head, but the knowledge was not yet welcome in my heart.

My head was saying, "Yeah, summer's here! The summer you've been waiting for! This is the summer that you build your log cabin! The summer your dream comes true!"

But there was still an ache in my heart that said, "It won't be the same without Kelly. I wonder if we should sell our lake lot. It just won't be the same without Kelly."

I was still struggling with "giving thanks in everything."

In the weeks and months following Kelly's death, I had made some progress on the road to recovery. I had boarded the boat called faith and had started the journey to the other side of the river, but sometimes I encountered some pretty mammoth waves.

In April I said, "I suppose we can get the foundation poured at the cabin as soon as the frost is out of the ground."

But the prospect didn't excite me. When I was a child, my family and I had spent one of our vacations in a log cabin on the Yellowstone River in Wyoming. We had a marvelous time, and I have never forgotten it. My dream had always been to have a log cabin of my own some day, my personal retreat from the rat race that life can be. Our plans for our cabin were well under way when Kelly died, and we had already invested a considerable amount of time and money in the project. If the logs hadn't already been cut, I think we might have canceled the project.

In April, just a month after Kelly's death, Mary and I were on the road to our spot on North Long Lake. Although we were building a new cabin, we had owned the lake lot with an old cabin for several years. Our family headed to the lake each weekend. Kelly, being the youngest, had spent far more time at the lake than his older brothers. He had loved it there. School friends often accompanied him to the lake, and they enjoyed water skiing and swimming.

Although Mary and I didn't say it, we knew this first trip to the lake would be very difficult.

"Remember how Kelly would get up in the morning and yell 'last one in is a chicken'? Then he would run out of the cabin, jump off the dock and into the lake."

"I remember," I said. "It sure was a morning eye-opener."

We drove along, the tears gently rolling down our cheeks.

Twenty minutes north of Brainerd, home of Paul Bunyan and Babe the Blue Ox, we pulled into our lake lot. We sat in the car for a few minutes and just looked out at the lake, each of us reliving whichever memories came to our minds.

"Reuel and Mary, welcome back! Did you have a nice winter?" Mark, our neighbor at the lake, came to greet us. As he walked across the yard, I realized that we had not notified him of Kelly's death. He was a good friend, a part of our family at the lake. He had watched our children grow up there. He loved our kids, and they loved him. Why hadn't anyone thought of calling Mark?

We talked with him for a few minutes, and then Mary told him about Kelly. As she did, the tears ran down Mark's face. Another wave, another passage.

After a few weeks, the foundation was poured, the logs were raised, and the walls were put in place. While I was up on the roof nailing shingles, I stopped to look at the lake. It was like a mirror, beautiful and serene that morning. A mother loon and her babies swam by in orderly procession. Suddenly the quiet was broken by a speedboat towing a slalom skier who threw a great wall of water as he cut across the wake behind the boat. My heart jumped for a moment. *Is that Kelly?* Then I was angry at myself that I could still have such thoughts. *But Kelly was a great skier,* I said to myself. I pictured him behind the boat, me at the wheel, Kelly dropping one ski, then spraying water on everyone at the dock!

I stood with the hammer in my hand, crying, staring out at the lake for several minutes until I grabbed another nail and beat it through a shingle.

I am no longer ashamed of these tears. They cleanse a part of my soul. They offer a marvelous release. I have learned that it is okay to cry.

One morning at the lake, I got out of bed and stood at a large window looking out across the water. A beautiful day. *A great day for a bike ride,* I thought. I had long known that exercise made me feel better, and I felt good when I exerted the self-discipline necessary to go biking or running. Bicycling had become my exercise of choice, and I especially loved biking at the lake because there were so many beautiful trails and roads. A few of the roads seemed like tunnels hollowed out of the pines trees that lined their shoulders, and I loved speeding through them. I was on my bike and racing through the woods before the sun got out of bed.

I was pushing myself extra hard that morning, my heart beating rapidly, the blood rushing to my face. I looked at the odometer on the handle bars: twenty-five miles so far. I pedaled on, my heart beating faster.

As the miles passed beneath my tires, memories raced through my mind—and with the memories came the questions. "Why did Kelly have to die? God, why did you let it happen? God, why didn't you stop it? Oh, God! God!" Before I realized it, I was shouting at the top of my lungs. My scream echoed through the surrounding woods as I cursed my pain...and God who allowed it.

I was immediately embarrassed and felt guilty about what I had done and said. At least no one heard me. No one, that is, except God. Where had that anger come from? And who was I angry at?

At last I admitted it. "I'm angry at you, God. I wonder, at times, if you even exist. Or if you do exist, do you really care? You say you're closest to people when they need you the most. Well, if that's the case, where are you right now? Why don't you take away my hurt? Where are you, God? Where? Show me that you haven't deserted me, God. I need a sign!"

It was the most honest prayer I'd ever prayed.

I stopped pedaling momentarily as I banked to take the corner ahead of me. Rounding the corner, I noticed three bikers ahead of me. One of the bicycles was pulling a little bike trailer. In big letters on the back of the trailer was painted the phrase, JESUS IS LORD!

God, you are awesome, I thought. He had immediately answered my prayer. When I prayed for a sign, I didn't know God would send an actual sign!

I sped up, rode alongside the trio, and said hello.

Friendly smiles greeted me, obviously happy to encounter a fellow cyclist. "Good morning. Gorgeous day, isn't it?"

"It sure is," I answered. "Where are you guys from?"

"Oregon."

"Oregon! You've biked all the way here from Oregon?"

"Yeah, we are on our way to Connecticut. We figure we'll get there in late August."

"Wow, that's quite a trip. I see the guitar strapped to your trailer. Do you guys sing or something?"

"Well, you see, we're Christians, and each night we find a campground, pitch our tent and build a fire, and then meet our neighbors. Then we get out the guitar and start to sing a few songs around the campfire, inviting other campers to come join us. Soon we start to sing gospel songs, and we share our faith in Jesus. It's incredible the opportunities God gives us to minister."

"That really is great," I said. "I'm a believer, too."

"Praise the Lord!" the trio answered simultaneously.

We rode and talked for a few more moments, and then one of the bikers asked, "Where is a good place to eat breakfast?"

"If you don't mind toast and cold cereal, you're welcome to join me. My cabin is quite close."

"We'd love to."

After a breakfast of toast and Wheaties, we sat

in my living room for over two hours and shared our mutual faith. Before they left, we prayed together. It was a very moving time. I stood watching them as they rode out my driveway, the words JESUS IS LORD! slipping from view as the trailer and the bikers rounded the corner and were lost behind the trees.

I couldn't help but think of the verse from Hebrews that reads: "Do not neglect to show hospitality to strangers, for by this some have entertained angels without knowing it" (Hebrews 13:2). I doubt that the bikers were angels, but they might as well have been. I thanked God for bringing us together for such a special time.

When I told Mary about the experience, she asked, "Did you tell them about Kelly?"

"I never mentioned it," I said, "nor did I tell them about my angry outburst or my desperate call to God."

"Why not?"

"It wasn't necessary. Their presence alone was God's sign to me that he really does care and he is with me."

❖ ❖

By the end of the summer, the cabin was almost finished. Working on it had been a blessing, despite the many tears that we shed there. Each log we raised and each nail we pounded were signals that we were moving forward with our lives.

One day, as the cabin neared completion, Mary

and I realized we had worked for about ten hours straight without stopping. "Better get something to eat," Mary said. As we ate supper it was obvious from our conversation we were excited about finishing the cabin, although melancholy that Kelly would never enjoy it with us.

After supper we walked down to the end of dock and then sat and enjoyed the sunset over North Long. Soon the stars were out, and Mary and I lingered on the dock, sharing feelings inspired by nature's beauty.

"Isn't the sky spectacular tonight?" I asked.

"It's breathtaking."

"I feel almost guilty for enjoying it. Sometimes I wonder if I am allowed to enjoy anything anymore."

"I feel the same way," Mary said.

"Will life ever be really enjoyable again?"

"Life will never be the same. We'll always be reminded of Kelly."

"But that doesn't mean that we can't enjoy life, does it?"

Mary said it so well. "I guess we have a choice, Reuel. We can choose to allow Kelly's death to destroy us and our joy, or we can choose to make the best of it and go on with life and enjoy the many, many blessings that God has given us."

As we sat there that night looking at the heavens, we made a choice. We decided to go on.

"Mary, I realize now what the Bible means about being thankful in every situation. It's the difference between being thankful *for* everything and being thankful *in* all things. I don't think God really expects me to be happy that Kelly committed suicide, any more than I would be happy if I got cancer. But I can still give thanks in the middle of a bad situation. I can thank God for giving me the strength to endure. I can thank him for the promise of eternal life. I can thank God for all the other blessings he has given me. I can thank him for understanding my feelings, even my anger, knowing that his son died, too. I really do have much to thank God for." I paused. "And I'm especially thankful tonight for you, Mary."

She smiled that sweet smile of hers, the one that warms me to my toes. "I'm thankful, too, Reuel."

We took one last look at the stars and headed down the dock. "Isn't that one beautiful cabin?"

"It sure is. Just like we've always wanted."

Chapter Eleven

Seasons Change

I thought I could smell a bit of fall in the air as I measured the opening where the kitchen window would go. Maple trees change colors first, and I'd seen several brilliant orange ones the day before as I had biked down one of my favorite trails. A flock of Canadian geese had flown over me, so low to the ground that their honking was deafening. Mary and I would have the cabin nearly finished before the weather got too cold. As I reached for the window to fit it into the opening, I realized that I was thankful that we had gone ahead with our plans to build the cabin.

Seasons change. This is one of the things I love about Minnesota—and one of the things I love about life.

"Good afternoon, Reuel." I turned to see my neighbor, D. H. Shala, but I could tell from the sound of his voice that this wasn't a social call.

"I got a call from Gary, your neighbor in Plymouth. He wants you to call him right away at this number." D. H. handed me a slip of paper with the telephone number on it.

My heart skipped a beat. It had to be an emergency for Gary to call me at the lake. What had happened now? My mind raced with a thousand possible scenarios. *I hope Scott and Kent and their families are all okay,* I thought. *I hope our house burned down or something like that—as long as the kids are okay.* Most people would think that losing your house in a fire, a flood, or through some natural disaster would be a tragedy of significant proportions, and for those who experience it, it is. But since Kelly's death, material things had taken on a whole new perspective. Things can be replaced.

"You can use the phone at my house," D. H. said.

"Thanks." I quickly walked to D. H.'s house, picked up the phone, and unfolded the paper with the telephone number. It was not the number of our neighbor's house, and I wondered where I was calling.

Gary answered the phone.

"Gary, this is Reuel." I couldn't help but remember calling home from the Denver airport the night of Kelly's death and hearing Pastor Vawter's voice on the other end of the phone.

"Reuel," Gary said, "I'm at the hospital. Before I tell you what happened, I want you to know that everything is okay."

I was relieved and worried at the same time. If everything was okay, why was he at the hospital?

"Kent had a diving accident last night. He dove into a swimming pool and broke his neck. He's in traction, but he is fully conscious and he wants to talk to you. Just a minute and I'll put him on the phone."

I could picture Kent in the bed. I knew that broken necks often meant paralysis. I thought of Joni Eareckson and her fateful dive into Chesapeake Bay that left her completely paralyzed. I feared the worst for Kent.

"Hi, Dad." He sounded fine.

"Kent, tell me how you are."

"I'm okay, Dad, don't worry. I have a broken neck, but I can move everything, even my neck. I don't have any numbness, so that's a good sign. A neurosurgeon is coming to see me pretty soon, and he will give me the whole scoop. But I don't want you and Mom to worry. I'm okay."

I fought back the tears. "I'll get Mom, and we'll come right away. We should be there within three hours."

"Please don't worry, Dad. I'll be all right."

"I love you, Kent, and I'll be there as soon as I can."

"I love you, too, Dad."

I ran from D. H.'s house and met Mary coming toward me. Her expression asked the question. I told her everything I knew in one breath. "I told him that we'd be there within three hours, so we'd better go."

Instead of running for the car, we just stood and held each other for a moment and cried. "I don't know if I can take any more," Mary said.

"I don't know if I can either, Mary."

The two-and-a-half hour trip to Minneapolis seemed to take forever. "He sounded all right, but if he is in traction, it may be more serious that he's letting on."

Mary and I took turns making statements, our concerns and fears obvious in our remarks.

Haven't we experienced enough tragedy in our lives? I wondered. How could God allow this to happen to us after all we've been through?

After what seemed an eternity, we pulled into the parking lot of North Memorial Hospital in Minneapolis.

The picture of Kent in the Stryker bed with tongs screwed into his head will forever be etched in my mind. Mary and I walked to his bed, trying hard to be strong. We each took hold of one of Kent's hands.

"What exactly happened, Kent?"

"Some buddies and I were staying at a hotel in Alexandria, and we were swimming in the pool. I took a dive into the pool and hit my head on the bottom. I felt a lot of pain, and I thought I might have whiplash. I was able to get out of the pool and go back to my room and lie down on the bed."

"Did you dive into the shallow end?"

"No, off the deep end, but I still hit the bottom."

"How did you find out your neck was broken?"

"Well, the pain was unbearable. I kept thinking that if I could just get to sleep, I'd feel better in the morning. But when morning came, I couldn't even get out of bed."

"So what did you do?"

"A couple of my buddies each grabbed an arm and pulled me upright. I could stand okay. I tried to take a shower, but the pain was so intense that I couldn't stand the water hitting my head. Finally I told my friends that I thought they'd better take me to the hospital."

"You should have gone to the hospital right away," I said.

"Yeah, I realize that now, but I kept thinking it was going to get better. Anyway, I was able to walk into the emergency room. They admitted me right away and took some x-rays. I have a severe fracture of the fifth vertebrae."

"Thank God you're not paralyzed."

"The doctors in Alexandria thought I should be transferred here, so they brought me here by ambulance."

"Oh, Kent..." Mary and I just stood by his bed for a minute and held his hands.

After leaving Kent's room, we were both anxious to talk with the neurosurgeon. What he told us both frightened us and made us extremely thankful.

"Your son is one lucky young man. When I walked into his room and saw him lying face down feeding himself, I could hardly believe it. I had viewed his x-rays and figured I was going to be visiting a quadriplegic. The fracture is so severe I was certain the spinal cord must be damaged. The fact that he still has movement is nothing short of miraculous. One wrong move could have caused the fracture to sever his spinal column."

"Oh, thank God," was all we could say.

"But surgery will be necessary."

"What type of surgery?"

"We will make these incisions. One incision will be made in the front of the neck so that a bone graft can be applied to the front side of the vertebrae. A second incision will be made in the hip. From the hip we will take the bone which we will graft to the vertebrae."

As the doctor explained the procedure, I realized that Kent was not out of danger yet. The operation might not be successful. Mary and I listened intently as the doctor continued to explain the procedure.

"We will make a third incision in the back of the neck. Here we will clamp the fourth, fifth, and sixth vertebrae together. Then we will sew him back up. Kent will have to wear a halo for several weeks, but after a few months, if the surgery is successful, he should be as good as new."

If the surgery is successful . . . I heard the words

over and over again. *Dear God, please help the surgery be successful. I can't bear the thought of Kent being paralyzed.*

"We've scheduled the surgery for tomorrow morning at 11:00. The procedure should take about six hours. Will you be present?"

"Of course we will," Mary and I answered in unison.

"I will come out about halfway through the surgery and let you know how it is going. Do you have any questions?"

"No, thank you, Doctor. Our prayers will be with you."

"I appreciate that," he said.

And they were. Mary and I prayed together that evening, and we enlisted the prayer support of other family and friends as well. The whole time we sat in the surgery waiting room, with time going by at a snail's pace, we prayed. We prayed for the doctor's skill, as well as for a successful surgery.

Three hours came and went. *Shouldn't the surgery be half over? Shouldn't the doctor be giving us the half-time report?*

Another half hour dragged by.

Mary and I saw the doctor at the same time. He came walking toward us, removing the mask from his face. We anxiously waited for the initial verdict.

"The bone graft went very well. We are half-way through the procedure. Next we will be installing the clamp on the fourth, fifth, and sixth vertebrae."

"But the graft went well?" I asked, in need of more assurance.

"Very well," the surgeon reiterated.

"Thank God," Mary and I said together. Then as the doctor turned and headed back for the operating room, we returned to the unpleasant task of filling time in the waiting room.

Another hour passed.

Two hours.

Three more hours.

After a total of seven hours, the doctor emerged from the operating room. Both Mary and I held our breath as we waited to hear his report. *Why had the operation lasted so much longer than they had anticipated? What had gone wrong?*

The surgeon spoke: "Kent will be in the recovery room for at least another half hour. Then you can see him. He will be in a lot of pain and will be heavily sedated, so you will want to keep your visit short. The surgery went very well, and he should recover completely."

"Oh, thank you, Doctor! Thank you so much!" And as the doctor walked away, we thanked God as well.

Kent was still in the recovery room when we first saw him. He was in immense pain. He didn't want us to leave him. I remember thinking to myself, "Yes, you'll always be a child to me, Kent. No matter how old or how big you get, you'll always be my son, and I'll always love you."

Once Kent had been moved to his room, Mary and I sat beside his bed, massaging his back and rubbing his arms. We didn't do much talking, but words were not necessary. Many times one's presence says more than words. Our presence was soothing for Kent.

After Kent was sound asleep, we left to go home. We were mentally and physically drained. But the surgery had been a success. Thank God!

Suddenly a tough question hit me. Would I have thanked God if the surgery had not been successful? Would I have blamed God for allowing Kent to break his neck, rendering him a quadriplegic? Would my faith have failed me if one tragedy had been added to another? So many of the feelings that I worked through after Kelly's death came rushing back.

I was aware of the pain again, and it directed me to God. "God, you really want to break me, don't you?"

The answer I felt from God surprised me. "No, Reuel, I don't want to break you. I want to make you into the mature man of God I want you to be. Just as Kent will always be your child, you are mine. And I want what's best for you."

Remember, Reuel, don't lose *your faith*—use *your faith!*

Kelly's death taught us that tragic things do happen to Christian people. We are not exempt from the pain and the suffering of the world. God has not promised us a life without trial. Kent's near-paralyzing accident taught us that just because one tragic event occurs in our lives, we are not necessarily guaranteed that something else tragic won't happen. Nonetheless, through it all God is faithful. He can turn tragedy into triumph. And pain is the path that leads us to the most intimate relationship with him.

Kent's recovery was long and complex, but he did recover—without any paralysis and with greater personal and emotional strength. And Kent's experience also drew me even closer to God, made me more conscious of the need for complete reliance on him. This experience, along with Kelly's death, has refined my faith. The Bible assures us that this is what suffering does:

> *Blessed be the God and Father of our Lord Jesus Christ, who according to his great mercy has caused us to be born again to a living hope through the resurrection of Jesus Christ from the dead, to obtain an inheritance which is imperishable and undefiled and will not fade away, reserved in heaven for you, who are protected by the power of God through faith for a salvation ready to be revealed in the last time.*
>
> *In this you greatly rejoice, even though now for a little while, if necessary, you have been distressed by various trials, that the*

> *proof of your faith, being more precious than gold which is perishable, even though tested by fire, may be found to result in praise and glory and honor at the revelation of Jesus Christ. (1 Peter 1:3-7)*

I know that my faith has, indeed, been tested by fire. I thank God for the trials that have come my way, for they have helped purify my faith. This Scripture tells us that our faith is far more precious to God than gold: "If your faith remains strong after being tried in the test tube of fiery trials, it will bring you much praise and glory and honor on the day of his return" (1 Peter 1:7 TLB).

Mary and I have walked through some deep valleys, and we know that there may be more ahead. We also know that no matter what, God will always be there with us. Nothing can separate us from his love.

> *Who shall separate us from the love of Christ? Shall tribulation, or distress, or persecution, or famine, or nakedness, or peril, or sword?*
>
> *Just as it is written,*
> *"FOR THY SAKE WE ARE BEING PUT*
> *TO DEATH ALL DAY LONG;*
> *WE WERE CONSIDERED AS SHEEP TO*
> *BE SLAUGHTERED."*
> *But in all these things we overwhelmingly*

conquer through him who loved us.

For I am convinced that neither death, nor life, nor angels, nor principalities, nor things present, nor things to come, nor powers, nor height, nor depth, nor any other created thing, shall be able to separate us from the love of God, which in Christ Jesus our Lord.(Romans 8:35-39)

Nothing can separate us from the love of Christ—not suicide, not broken necks, not old age! Nothing can separate us from the love of Christ. Mary and I know this for a fact.

❖ ❖

We're going up to the cabin this weekend. It is fall again. The leaves are at their peak, and the forests are alive with color. Most lake residents have taken in their docks, and most of the snowbirds, those who head south to Florida or Arizona for the winter, have already flown away, along with the robins who haven't been seen for several weeks. Although it is only October, we've already seen a snowflake or two.

Seasons change, and I thank God that they do.

Chapter Twelve

With All the Loving and Caring He Has Shown

It has been six years since Kelly died. There *is* joy again, although I'll never be completely free of the pain. But that's okay. Pain is a pathway to a closer, deeper relationship with God. I know now that nothing can come my way that God and I can't handle together. Along with Paul I've said many times, "I can do all things through Christ who strengthens me" (Philippians 4:13).

God continues to open doors for me to minister, to be a comfort to others. Every few weeks I hear of some other family that has been visited by tragedy, often a suicide, and when possible, I try to be there. Whenever I do, I think about the simple advice that my father gave me many years ago: "Reuel, be there for someone." I did not know at the time how prophetic his words would be. God has engineered the circumstances of my life to give me a ministry of "being there" for others. And I never could have been or would have been if I hadn't lived through this loss. God does turn tragedy into triumph.

The night Mary and I sat beside Kent's bed, rubbing his back and legs, I was struck by the fact that no matter how old my children should ever become, they will always be my children; I will always have a father's heart. I have come to realize that likewise, no matter how old I become, I will always be a child of God. He will always love me with a Father's heart.

The pain I've encountered in my life changed my focus. I realize I need God's help each day, and each day I pray, "Dear Father, help me to comfort others in the same way you've comforted me." I fail occasionally, fragile as I am, but God is still there.

A few weeks ago I was going through an old box in the closet, and I rediscovered an essay that Kelly had written for a sophomore English class in high school. The assignment had been to write about the person who had been the greatest influence in your life. Kelly wrote:

> *The person who I think had the most influence on my life has been my father. He has always been there when I needed him, whether it was for advice or just to listen to me. He has taught me right from wrong, although I haven't always listened. He has also helped me through some rough times by*

encouraging and backing me up.

My father has supported me through many activities, such as scouts, hockey, school, and all other activities. He has made me respect myself as well as him.

I would like to live my life as my father has lived his, with all the love, caring, and responsibility he has shown.

Kelly, the greatest tribute I can pay you is to live life to the fullest, to live in such a manner as to bring honor and glory to God. Your life will forever be a part of mine. Until we're together again, I want to live my life as Christ did his, with all the love, caring, and responsibility he has shown.

I Love You, Kelly.
Dad.

EPILOGUE

Depression is a brain disease caused by a chemical change in the brain. If unrecognized and untreated, major depression can lead to suicide.

A person showing signs of depression needs to see a medical doctor or psychiatrist. Medicine is available to treat major depression, manic depression, and other disorders, and only a doctor can prescribe those medications.

Serious depression is often a hidden disease. It appears as unhappiness about life's problems. People who suffer from it go to school, hold jobs, and fulfill their responsibilities. They don't look or act sick, but they carry the tremendous burden of invisible pain.

Some of the signs of depression are:

- Sad or empty moods much of the time
- Feelings of hopelessness or helplessness

- Pessimism
- Feelings of guilt or worthlessness
- Feelings of failure
- Fatigue
- Loss of interest in everyday activities
- Decreased interest in sex
- Eating too much or too little
- Sleeping disorders
- Restlessness
- Irritability
- Difficulty in concentrating
- Large and sudden mood swings
- Distancing themselves from family and friends
- Suicidal thoughts or plans

If a person has four or more of these symptoms, he or she should see a doctor or psychiatrist immediately.

To the untrained observer, these symptoms can appear to be deliberate—things that you could expect a person to correct on his or her own. The depressed person cannot change these symptoms without medication to correct the chemical imbalance that has taken place in the brain. Without professional medical help, depression can lead to suicide.

Danger signs of suicide include:

- Talking about suicide
- Statements of hopelessness or worthlessness

- Preoccupation with death
- Loss of interest in things one cares for
- A sudden happier or calmer mood
- Suddenly visiting or calling persons one cares about
- Making arrangements, setting one's affairs in order
- Giving away personal belongings

A suicidal person urgently needs to see a doctor or psychiatrist.

Misunderstanding about depression and suicide is widespread. Some think that people who have brain diseases and people who kill themselves are bad or weak or sinful. The truth is, these people are suffering from an illness—like diabetes or other diseases—that can be medically treated.

The grief and frustration of this tragedy have changed my life forever, have put the meaning of life into a new perspective. The day-to-day struggles of my life are trivial in comparison to the loss of my son. Mary and I have been drawn closer together. Neither of us knows what tomorrow will bring, but we thank God for today and know that he can now use us in a way that he could not have done before.

